# ARE MY
*Prayers*
## FALLING
## ON
## DEAF
## EARS?

# ARE MY *Prayers* FALLING ON DEAF EARS?

A Biblical Scholar Takes
a Personal Look at Prayer

*by Dr. Andrew Steinmann*

Grand Rapids, Michigan 49418 USA

Cover design by JMK & Associates, Grand Rapids, MI.
Interior design by Pinpoint Marketing, Kirkland, WA.
Edited by Judy Bodmer and Heather Stroobosscher.

ISBN 0-529-10742-2

Library of Congress Catalog Card Number 96-061530

*Printed in the United States of America*

1 2 3 4 5 6 7   01 00 99 98 97

*For everyone who prayed for me*
*and for all who prayed with me.*

# Contents

# Forward

WROTE THIS BOOK during a time that challenged me not only to pray but also to examine prayer. I had lost my job. The part-time jobs I did find helped fill an economic need but left a spiritual void. I keenly felt that my God-given talents were not being used. I longed to have a job that would enable me to help provide for my family and also provide a meaningful way to use the talents I felt God had given me. In other words, I needed more than employment. I needed a vocation.

This need moved me to prayer. I prayed for many things, but above all else I prayed about my desire for a job that would be a vocation. At times it seemed as if God did not, could not, or would not hear my prayers. I was confident that he listened, but I saw little tangible evidence of his attention to the needs that I felt most.

Prayer had been a part of my life since my childhood when my parents taught me to pray, showed me how to pray, and took me to church to pray. Yet, the experience of prayer during this challenging period of my life has led me a to deeper appreciation of the privilege of prayer that God has given to his people. This book is a collection of my thoughts, conclusions, and reflections on some of the prayers in the Bible.

# *1*

# *When God Is Deaf*

*RAYER CAN BE* a lonely experience. While some prayers are said in groups, around a table before a meal, during worship, or before a meeting of a religious organization, most prayer are spontaneous, informal, unrehearsed thoughts brought to God by individuals.

In my work as a pastor at a nursing home, I have witnessed the lonely side of prayer. Many of the residents are confined to bed with little chance to do much except perhaps watch television or listen to the radio. They spend a lot of time praying about their condition, their family and friends, and other concerns. Yet, every time I stop by to visit with them, it seems that the most special time is the time we spend praying together. They appreciate having a chance to pray with someone so much that they will thank me for stopping by to *pray* with them. We may have talked, read the Bible, shared some common interest together, but the time spent in prayer is the most important part of my visit because it removes the loneliness from prayer.

When a concern dominates our thoughts for days or even weeks, we pray frequently about it. Privately we share our most personal desires and thoughts with God. But, of course, we cannot see, feel, or hear him as we can our fellow humans. Talking to a close friend, a parent, a spouse, or even a therapist can have a healing effect because we get instant feedback, visually and orally. We may even receive a comforting embrace. Although God is the best friend we could ever have, we receive none of those healing gestures that another human being can give us.

If, on top of that, we do not perceive God is listening to our prayers or answering them, the loneliness of prayer can be devastating. We can feel as if we are lost in a wilderness without food or shelter, not knowing which way to turn and having no way of finding a path that will lead us out. When we feel as if we are praying to a God who doesn't hear, a God who has become deaf, prayer seems emptied of its meaning and purpose.

However, when we take the time to examine prayers in the Bible prayed by people who complained that God was not listening to them, we find that we are not alone in feeling this way. Moreover, when we examine these prayers we learn two lessons:

1.  Prayer does not begin with human effort to pester God until he listens. It begins with God's promise of mercy toward us.
2.  Prayer is not a way to manipulate God into answering our questions or solving our problems in the ways we want them solved. It is designed to help us transcend our problems and troubles by focusing on God.

## Psalm 113
### *Not a Way to Manipulate God*

Psalm 13 is a prayer that was spoken to God when it seemed that God was deaf.

> How long, O LORD? Will you forget me forever?
> How long will you hide your face from me?
> How long must I make decisions alone
>   with sorrow in my heart day after day?
> How long will my enemy triumph over me?
>
> Look at me! Answer me, O Lord my God!
> Light up my eyes,
>   or else I will die
>     and my enemy will say, "I have overpowered him."
>       My opponents will rejoice because I have been shaken.
>
> But I trust your mercy.
> My heart finds joy in your salvation.
> I will sing to the LORD because he has been good to me.

In this prayer the psalmist boldly confronts his God. This is a prayer of desperation and a prayer of trust. Desperation and trust may seem contradictory, but they coexist in this prayer. The psalmist has lost hope, wondering whether God has permanently forgotten him. God has seemingly gone into hiding. But God is not hiding from everyone. The composer of this prayer feels as if God is hiding only from him. After all, God is not with him to guide him with wise advice. In his sorrow of feeling abandoned, he feels a need for guidance from heaven. Yet no guidance is available. His prayers seem to go unanswered because they are not heard.

The psalmist's hopelessness turns into desperation as he cries out, "Look at me! Answer me . . ." He feels as if he is on the verge of

13

death, and those who caused his tragic state, the ones he calls enemies, will rejoice. They will have the joy of feeling they were right in doing whatever they did to make him miserable.

This prayer is one that could be prayed by anyone who feels others have wronged him and gotten away with it. The utter hopelessness of feeling one has lost something unjustly at the hands of someone else with no way of getting it back is devastating. Whether one has lost a job, health, prosperity, friends, or family, the thought of never recovering what was lost can immobilize and paralyze the strongest of persons. Television news reports often show a person who is grieving at the loss of a loved one who was needlessly killed. The grief of such people is almost too painful to watch as it is beamed into our homes. We know nothing will bring that lost loved one back. We can feel the sorrow, rage, and gloom of the person who is crying over their dead loved one. We can be filled with their righteous indignation as they call for justice to be done and the killers to be prosecuted and punished.

Yet, even though we can sympathize with such people as their stories are told to us through the flickering television screen, we cannot know the depth of their emotions until we experience a similar loss. Whether that loss is through death of a loved one or something less violent, such as a lost job, lost reputation, or lost friends, the grieving and hopelessness can be strikingly similar to the death of a loved one. And at times these are multiple losses. Losing a job can mean losing the friends one had made at the workplace. Losing one's reputation can also cost us friends and perhaps even a job or a career.

When such a loss occurs, our prayers, like the psalmist's prayer, can turn into cries of "how long?" How long is God going to allow me to suffer? Will this last for the rest of my life? Will I ever regain my job, reputation, friends, health, prosperity? Often we know that what we lost was lost forever. The happy situation we knew cannot be reconstructed. Like Humpty Dumpty, nothing, not even all the king's horses and all the king's men will ever put things back as they were. We often desire to have what we lost, but we know that is not what we will get.

However, the psalmist's prayer was one of trust as well as hopelessness. Note that he does not pray that God will give him what he lost. In faith he accepts that everything that happens to him is under God's control (Romans 8:28). God could restore his position, his reputation, his friends. But as much as the psalmist demands that God quit hiding and listen, he does not demand that God give him back what he lost. His faith transcends his loss. He will trust God.

God's mercy is the key to the psalmist's prayer. He says he has no right to demand anything. God owes him nothing. Yet, he knows that God will have mercy on him. The opponents who caused him loss and anguish may rejoice in overpowering him, but his joy is in God's salvation. It may not have been the salvation and vindication that the psalmist envisioned. Nevertheless, the psalmist knows that God's plan to save him from his despair is best—whether or not it conforms to his own plan.

The last line of this prayer is perhaps the most remarkable. The God who forgot the psalmist, the God who abandoned him to make decisions without spiritual guidance, is the God who has been good to the psalmist. Hopeless despair has turned into gratitude and praise. The desperate cries of a fallen man have become grateful songs.

Thus, we see the prayer is being answered before it has ended. God will continue to be merciful to him. The psalmist has not only received his answer, but that answer has also begun to change him before he gets to "amen."

This psalm teaches us our first important lesson about prayer: *Prayer does not begin with human effort to pester God until he listens. Prayer begins with God's promise of mercy toward us.* As much as the Bible tells us to pray often and always (Luke 18:1, 1 Thessalonians 5:17), it does not tell us that God listens to us more closely because we pray more often (Matthew 6:7).

Prayer is not the same as calling God on the telephone and letting it ring over and over again until he answers so that he doesn't have to listen to the ringer any more. Instead, prayer is the response we have to God's promise to have mercy on us. Because we know that he is merciful, we pray. Even when he appears to be deaf and cannot or will not hear us, we trust his promise of mercy. In fact, God answered the psalmist's prayer by allowing him to realize God's mercy toward him.

The same realization that the psalmist had moves us to pray, even when we think God is deaf and doesn't hear. We trust that God is merciful and will be as good to us as he was to the psalmist. That is why we continue to pray even though God appears to be deaf (see Luke 18:7-8).

## Psalm 77
## *Where Can We Find Comfort?*

Another psalm that was prayed to God when he appeared to be deaf is Psalm 77. This prayer is attributed to Asaph, the musician David appointed to lead worship in the tabernacle. Here the psalmist speaks of his inner feelings as he prays to God. Thus, this prayer helps us to come to grips with our feelings about praying to a deaf God:

Loudly, I cried to God.
Loudly, I cried to God
  so that he would open his ears to hear me.
On the day I was in trouble, I went to the Lord for help.
At night I stretched out my hands in prayer without
    growing tired.
  Yet, my soul refused to be comforted.

I sigh as I remember God.
I begin to lose hope as I think about him.                    *Selah*
  (You keep my eyelids open.)
I am so upset that I cannot speak.
I have considered the days of old,
    the years long ago.
I remember my song in the night
    and reflect on it.
My spirit searches for an answer:
  Will the Lord reject me for all time?
  Will he ever accept me?
  Has his mercy come to an end forever?
  Has his promise been canceled throughout every generation?
  Has God forgotten to be merciful?
  Has he locked up his compassion because of his anger? *Selah*
    Then I said, "It makes me feel sick
      that the power of the Most High is no longer the same."

I will remember the deeds of the LORD.
I will remember your ancient miracles.
I will reflect on all your actions
    and think about what you have done.

O God, your ways are holy!
  What god is as great as our God?
You are the God who performs miracles.
You have made your strength known among the nations.

With your might you have defended your people,
the descendants of Jacob and Joseph. *Selah*

The water saw you, O God.
The water saw you and shook.
Even the depths of the sea trembled.
The clouds poured out water.
The sky thundered.
Even your arrows flashed in every direction.
The sound of your thunder rumbled in the sky.
Streaks of lightning lit up the world.
The earth trembled and shook.

Your road went through the sea.
Your path went through raging water,
but your footprints could not be seen.
Like a shepherd, you led your people.
You had Moses and Aaron take them by the hand.

This interesting prayer expresses the emotional turmoil that many people feel as they pray to God when they have trouble, and they cannot sense any response from him. Although we have no clue what that trouble was, we know the psalmist went to God with it. Perhaps he had in mind the promise made by God in Psalm 50, another of the psalms of Asaph: "Call on me in times of trouble. I will rescue you, and you will honor me" (Psalm 50:15).

Whatever trouble the psalmist found himself in, this prayer reveals it occupied all his thoughts. We do not know what the psalmist's friends and families thought of his preoccupation with his troubles. They may have been supportive. On the other hand, they may have thought it was silly. We have all had that experience. Something is troubling us. Others counsel us to forget the matter. They tell us it's not worth losing sleep over. (Notice that the psalmist said he was praying at night and his eyelids did not close.) Even if it's not important to others, it's important to us. In those cases the only place we can go is to God.

That is exactly what the psalmist did. He prayed with the normal posture of prayer in his day. Instead of folding his hands and bowing his head as we often do, he stretched out his arms and most likely looked upward toward heaven. In this position he shouted his prayer to God. His prayers must have been tiring, both physically and emotionally. It's not easy to keep one's arms extended for long periods of time and even harder to do it while speaking loudly. Yet, he did not tire.

Psychologically, God's deafness to his prayer was taking its toll. He had no inner comfort that came as a result of his prayer. He speaks of losing hope. He tells us that he was so upset that he could no longer speak. Physically, he was able to stretch out his hands in prayer. However, he was so mentally and emotionally drained he couldn't sleep, and he could no longer speak his prayers. He blames God for keeping his eyelids open and not bringing sleep. Perhaps he means that God, by not answering his prayer the way the psalmist desired, was the cause of his insomnia.

I know what this prayer is speaking about. When I was young, my cares and troubles rarely, if ever, kept me awake at night. I had little to worry about and even less to lose. As a child I was confident my parents would take care of my troubles. As a young man I had only myself to worry about. But as I grew older and took on the responsibilities of a husband and father, and as I was given the additional responsibilities of a job, I found that my troubles kept me awake at night. I would fall asleep, only to find myself wide awake in the middle of the night. I would toss and turn, finally get up, and try to forget my troubles by watching the feeble offerings of late night television or by praying and meditating on the Bible. And often, like the psalmist, I could not speak a prayer from my state of mental exhaustion.

Because the psalmist was unable to sleep, his mind became focused on God's past actions. He remembered what God had done for Israel, and he remembered when he had joyfully sung to God during the night. Now, during this night of worry and distress, he searched back through God's historical relationship with his people and his own relationship with God and asked if these held the answers to his questions.

This prayer is full of questions that must have run through the psalmist's mind. Could he trust God to keep his promise of mercy? The implication of this question is that the psalmist had a preconceived notion of *how* God's mercy would affect his life. He not only wanted God's mercy, but he wanted his mercy to be shown in a certain way. If God would just do the thing the psalmist wanted and solve his difficulties in the way the psalmist thought best, he would know God was merciful.

Moreover, the psalmist's questions are signs of his impatience with God. When he asks whether God will ever accept him, he is implying he not only knows how God should solve his problem, but he also knows when God should do it: *immediately!*

Many of the questions we have in times of trouble are not the same questions that the psalmist asked. We want to know why God has allowed us to be in the situation we're in. One popular book published several years ago was titled *When Bad Things Happen to Good People*. We especially want to know *why* bad things happen to us, because we must be part of those good people the book title was speaking of. We ask ourselves, "Why is this happening to me? Why did God allow this to affect me (or someone I care about)?"

Like the psalmist our question of why something happened to us is often never answered. Indeed, knowing why would not make our troubles less troublesome. Knowing why would not allow us to cope any better with them. Though we seek to know why God allows a certain trouble to enter our life, knowing why is not the answer. Even if we could understand God's reasons, we would still need a solution to our troubles. Knowing why will not comfort us, no matter how much we think it will.

What will comfort us? The psalmist thought about the things God had done for his people in the past. Instead of using those ancient acts of God as a way to detect answers to the questions that plagued him, he found comfort in them. The comfort he found was the answer to his prayer. He discovered that God led his people like a shepherd. Shepherds don't attempt to reason with their sheep or answer their sheep's questions. The sheep wouldn't understand the answers if they had them. What sheep need are wise leadership and protection. Sheep cannot fully understand what their shepherd does or why he does it. However, they can learn to trust the shepherd. (This insight alone can lead us to a greater appreciation of Psalm 23.)

That is what the psalmist learned as he reviewed Israel's history. He remembered God's miracles. He describes God's power at the Red Sea when he made a path through the raging waters. The people of Israel knew they were in trouble when the Egyptian armies were bearing down on them. They may have questioned why God put them in the trouble they found themselves. They thought they had a good solution to their problem, and Moses (and God) should adopt that solution (see Exodus 14:12). But they didn't really know what was best. God's solution was provided through Aaron and Moses when the Red Sea parted and they crossed.

The psalmist recognized that his comfort came in trusting God's way of doing things. He rejoiced that God's ways are holy. He also noted that God created a path of escape through the sea for his people. However, God's footprints could not be seen. The people had to trust God was leading them and would not let the sea collapse in on them. Instead of seeing evidence God was saving them, they had to trust he would save them.

The New Testament also shows us this working of God in the crucifixion of Jesus. Throughout Jesus' arrest, trial, and crucifixion, we cannot see God's power forcefully at work. Instead, God in the person of Jesus appears to be at the mercy of the Jewish leaders, the crowd, the Roman soldiers, and Pontius Pilate. The only footprints to follow are the footprints of a condemned man carrying a cross. God's power appears to be absent as he is beaten, mocked, rejected, and as he dies a horrible death. The people at the foot of the cross taunt Jesus and remind him that he said he trusted in God. Where was God to save him now? (Matthew 27:43).

Yet, the Bible makes clear God was most active in the crucifixion of Christ. In this apparent display of weakness, God was leading his people out of death and sin just as he led them out of Egypt.

God calls on us to trust we are saved by the death of Jesus. The people of Israel had to trust that the sea would not collapse around them, that they would be led to freedom and not to their deaths. We are to trust that in the cross of Christ we are led to freedom from sin and death. We are to trust that the same God who looked after his people at the Red Sea and who was there at the death of Jesus is not deaf to our prayers.

Many see the death of Christ as the death of a man, perhaps the unjust death of a very good man. But they do not see God at work in Jesus' death so that they might be saved from slavery to sin and death. Like the Egyptians who followed the Israelites into the sea and were drowned, they cannot see what only the person who trusts God knows—that in Jesus' death, he was at work to save his people. That same trust leads us to believe he is at work for us even when we think our prayers are falling on deaf ears. When God does not appear to be listening, he is still working for us. In prayer we focus on God, and we are reminded to trust him even when we cannot see his footprints.

The psalmist's comfort, then, was not in God answering his prayer by answering all his questions or by solving his problems in the way he thought God should solve them. His comfort was found in God himself. God was the answer to his prayer. He learned to trust his shepherd.

This prayer teaches us a second important lesson about prayer: *prayer is not a way to manipulate God into answering all our questions or solving our problems in the ways we want them solved. Prayer is designed to help us transcend our problems and troubles by focusing on God himself.* When God is deaf to our prayers, it is we who are unable to hear or understand. Our deafness makes him appear deaf. He seems deaf to our prayers because we don't want to be sheep that trust the shepherd. The shepherd knows more than we can understand. God's deafness is really our lack of trust in the one who has the power to defend his people and control the water, the clouds, the sky, thunder and lightning, the death of his Son, and the events in our life. Prayer allows us to focus on who God really is. It allows us to transcend our troubles even when it seems God is deaf.

In this chapter I have touched on only two prayers in the Bible. Both were prayed by people who were desperate for an answer and who thought God didn't to hear them. For further meditation, you may want to read some of the other ones. They include Psalms 10, 22, 44, 88, and 89. In addition, a number of psalms ask God not to hide from those who pray them. They beg God not to be deaf. These psalms do not exhibit the hopelessness of those who prayed the prayers examined in this chapter. Nevertheless, such psalms can also teach us about praying when God seems to be ignoring us. (For an example, see Psalm 28.)

# 2

# *When Evil Is Winning*

N THE YEAR 410, the Goth Alaric and his army conquered and sacked the city of Rome. For many
Christians this was a calamity without equal. The
great Roman empire that had been such an enemy of the church
in its formative years had been officially Christianized, and the
emperors had converted to the faith. Now the pagan Goths had
conquered Rome's empire. Many non-Christians in Rome blamed
its fall on the Christian religion. Not only did it seem that evil from
outside of Rome was winning the day, but also the evil inside the
city was vexing the church. In the midst of all this, Augustine, bish-
op of Hippo in North Africa, wrote his book *The City of God.* In
this book Augustine argues that no human city or government
should be equated with God, his church, or with victory over evil.
Cities built by humans will pass away, Augustine argued, but God's
eternal city, the New Jerusalem, will be the hope of Christians even
when evil seems to overcome good in this life.

That answer to evil is good, but hard to accept if you are the one experiencing the effects of evil directly. It may have been possible for Augustine to write it from a distance as he looked at Rome. However, the Roman Christians, though they knew in their hearts that Augustine was right, nevertheless had to cope day-to-day with the evil that had come upon them. They were confronted by the evil around them that seemed to be triumphing over good. They chafed under its apparent victory and resented that the pagan hordes now were their masters and, in some cases, their tormentors.

We can look back on the fall of Rome from the perspective of Christians living some sixteen centuries later and know that evil did not triumph but that the church survived. Yet when something evil happens to us or those whom we care about, we have a much harder time taking the long view of things and simply trusting that God will work them out for our good. We want to know why evil seems to be winning. We may even pray that God would punish those who did the evil and rescue us from our pain and despair.

In this chapter we will consider three types of prayers that we can pray in response to evil when it touches our lives: We can pray that God would punish those who do evil. We can pray that God will bless us when we avoid evil and try to do good. And we can pray for those who do evil. In studying prayers from the Bible spoken by those who experienced the consequences of others' evil acts, we will learn two lessons:

1. It is not wrong to ask God to deal with evil, even to punish evil people. It is wrong, however, to expect God to make the result be one in which humans can see that good unambiguously triumphs over evil.

2. Our prayers can be proactive. They can ask God for blessings and for good to come from what we do.

## Psalm 137
## "God, Punish Those Who Do Evil"

By the rivers of Babylon, we sat down and cried
as we remembered Zion.
We hung our lyres on willow trees.
It was there that those who had captured us
demanded that we sing.
Those who guarded us wanted us to entertain them.
⌊They said,⌋ "Sing a song from Zion for us!"

How could we sing the LORD's song in a foreign land?
If I forget you, Jerusalem,
let my right hand forget ⌊how to play the lyre.⌋
Let my tongue stick to the roof of my mouth
if I don't remember you,
if I don't consider Jerusalem my highest joy.

O LORD, remember the people of Edom.
Remember what they did the day Jerusalem was captured.
They said, "Tear it down! Tear it down to its foundation."
You destructive people of Babylon,
blessed is the one who pays you back
with the same treatment you gave us.
Blessed is the one who grabs your little children
and smashes them against a rock.

(Psalm 137)

We can hardly imagine the bitterness in the hearts of the first Judeans who prayed Psalm 137. Their experience has some parallels to modern people. Their homeland was attacked, overrun, and conquered by the Babylonians, a ruthless, destructive people. Similar things have occurred to many people in this century. During the siege of Judah's capital city, Jerusalem, many had to watch in horror as their children and elderly starved to death or slowly wasted away from disease. We have seen similar scenes of children with bloated, but empty stomachs who are innocent victims of war. The Judeans were forced into exile in a foreign land. In recent years refugees from numerous wars strain the most modern means of providing humanitarian aid. Our television documents the suffering in painful detail.

However, the comparisons of the Judeans' experience to modern experience tend to fade when we consider the other things they suffered at the hand of the Babylonians. The Israelites were forced to live in the land of their conquerors, who destroyed their land, enslaved them, and killed their husbands, uncles, and brothers. Moreover, their captors taunted them by demanding, "Sing a song from Zion for us." That request may seem innocent enough today, but it was a religious taunt to those who first prayed Psalm 137. To understand why, we must understand the religious ideology of ancient warfare in the Middle East.

When a king went to war against his neighbors, he believed that his god went with him and fought with him against the opposing king's god. Victory was viewed not only as the king's victory, but also as the victory of his god. Many times the conquered people were forced to adopt the conquering god as their own.

Against this background we should picture the people of Judah who remained faithful to their God. They acknowledged and worshipped only one God—the God of their ancestors Abraham, Isaac, and Jacob, the God of Moses, and their greatest king, David. No other god existed. Yet the Babylonians claimed their god had defeated Israel's God. He had been proven greater. The Judeans who refused to admit the superiority of Babylon and its gods were taunted by their captors. "Sing a song about Zion" was a request intended to remind the conquered Judeans of their God's inability to defend and of the destruction of their God's city. The Babylonians were going to ridicule these peculiar people who did not acknowledge what the whole world knew—the god of the conquering people is greater than the god of the conquered people.

To make matters more painful, Judah's neighbor Edom had joined the Babylonians in destroying Jerusalem. They cheered for its destruction. The descendants of Jacob's brother, Esau, who had sold his birthright and despised God's blessing, triumphed with the Babylonians.

Under such bitter conditions, how could the Judeans sing about Zion, the great city of their God? How could they sing with the joy they formerly had? Yet, they were determined not to forget their God and the joy of worshipping him in Jerusalem. Their bitterness would not keep them from singing to him. The taunts of their captors would not dim their faith in only one God, the one they had worshipped on Mount Zion.

The evil of the Babylonians had prevailed. The evils of their warfare had reduced Judah to rubble and its people to oppression. The god of Babylon appeared to be spiritually superior. How were the Judeans to pray under these circumstances? What were they to ask of God?

The request in Psalm 137 seems shocking to us: "You destructive people of Babylon, blessed is the one who pays you back with the same treatment you gave us. Blessed is the one who grabs your little children and smashes them against a rock" (8-9). How could this be in the same Bible as the advice "Love your enemies, and pray for those who persecute you" (Matthew 5:44)? Is this a proper prayer when evil and evildoers triumph in this world?

Perhaps the hardest prayers are those we pray when people who have done something morally wrong have prevailed over those who did what was right. When evil wins, something seems wrong. In the movies, on television, and in books our sense of morality is played out time and again. The good guys usually win the ultimate victory and are vindicated in the end. Sometimes they win in real life. But many times it is the ruthless use of power and authority that wins. At times that power resides in those who bend and break every moral precept but remain smugly self-righteous about themselves and their actions. Some get away with their immoral acts without ever paying a price for them. Others pay a price that is insignificant compared to the pain and misery they brought to others.

In Greenfield Village in Dearborn, Michigan, stands a house that has been reconstructed and restored to its original state. Its first use was as the manor house of a plantation in the Old South. Behind it stands a smaller structure that was originally a building where slaves worked to make butter. A sign informs visitors that the slaves worked under terrible conditions to make butter for several generations of plantation owners. However, the slaves were not given any of the butter they made. They were not allowed to benefit from their labor. The owners of the plantation prospered while the slaves toiled. Several generations of owners enriched themselves at their slaves' expense without ever having been called to account for their harsh and uncaring treatment of their slaves (contrary to the Scriptures, see Ephesians 6:9 and Colossians 4:1).

When we see evil triumph in our world, we can understand how the Judeans placed a blessing on those who paid back the

Babylonians for their evil. Our sense of moral outrage at the triumph of evil can also cause us to cry out for the punishment of the evildoer. We rejoice in their suffering as much as the Judeans who prayed that someone would smash Babylon's children against a rock. But even as we do, the thought persists that such calls for vengeance may also be evil.

## Jeremiah and Habakkuk: Prophets Who Prayed for Vengeance

However, many prayers in the Bible call for God to punish those who have done something evil toward the person praying. When some men plotted to assassinate Jeremiah, he prayed:

> O LORD of Armies, you judge fairly
> and test motives and thoughts.
> I want to see you take revenge on them,
> because I've brought my case to you.
>
> (Jeremiah 11:20)

On other occasions he prayed:

> Put my persecutors to shame,
> but do not let me be put to shame.
> Terrify them,
> but do not let me be terrified.
> Bring the day of disaster on them,
> and destroy them completely.
>
> (Jeremiah 17:18)

> But the LORD of Armies examines the righteous.
> He sees their motives and thoughts.
> I want to see you take revenge on them,
> because I've brought my case to you.
>
> (Jeremiah 20:12)

And in perhaps his most powerful prayer for vengeance the prophet prayed:

Pay attention to me, O Lord,
and listen to what my accusers say.
Good should not be paid back with evil.
They dig a pit to take my life.
Remember how I stood in your presence and pleaded
for them
in order to turn your anger away from them.
Now, hand their children over to famine.
Pour out their ⌊blood⌋ by using your sword.
Then their wives will become childless widows.
Their husbands will be put to death.
Their young men will be struck down in battle.
Make them cry out from their homes
when you suddenly send troops against them,
because they dug a pit to catch me and hid snares
for my feet.
But you, O Lord, know that they plan to kill me.
Don't forgive their crimes.
Don't wipe their sins out of your sight.
Make them stumble in your presence.
Deal with them when you get angry.
(Jeremiah 18:19-23)

Jeremiah's prayers request severe punishment for those who tried to harm him. He wants God to terrify them, to destroy them, to punish their wives, husbands, and children, and to refuse them any forgiveness. Moreover, Jeremiah is not alone in praying that God would undo the triumphant evil that harmed him. David prayed that God would make it possible for him to defeat Absolom (2 Samuel 15:31). Nehemiah prayed that God would not forget what his enemies had done (Nehemiah 6:14) and that God would not forget the sins of the priests who had brought dishonor on their holy office (Nehemiah 13:29).

We can try to explain Jeremiah's cries for violent vengeance as the result of the distress that he was under. We can claim that these prayers were applying the Old Testament rule of an eye-for-an-eye (Exodus 21:24, Leviticus 24:20, Deuteronomy 19:21) and do not apply to Christians who live under the New Testament (one example of an exception is Revelation 6:10). Yet we know that these are precisely the type of prayers we, too, are tempted to pray when someone harms us. They are especially attractive when we know that we did nothing wrong and that the harm is undeserved.

This fervor in calling for punishment for those who wronged others can be seen in the continuing outrage against surviving Nazis and Nazi collaborators from the Second World War. We are over fifty years distant from the atrocities committed in Germany. Most of those who worked with the Nazis have died, and those who are still alive are in their seventies or beyond. Yet, several governments still spend time and money to seek out and prosecute the few frail old men who committed those wicked deeds two generations ago. It is hard to give up the desire for vengeance even after half a century in the face of the terrible and unspeakable crimes that were committed against innocent people. Is it any wonder, then, that we also cling to vengeful emotions for injustices done to us personally?

Is it wrong to pray that God would execute justice against evil and those who do it, especially when evil appears to be winning? Or is it improper to pray that God would punish evil? Should we, perhaps, restrain from praying about vengeance for the evil that has touched our lives? If we answer yes to any of these questions we probably have to remove the book of Habakkuk from our Bibles. Habakkuk records three of his prayers asking God to punish those who do evil things. The first is Habakkuk 1:2-4:

How long, O LORD, am I to cry for help,
    but you will not listen?
I cry out to you, "There's violence!"
    yet you will not come to the rescue.
Why do you make me see wrongdoing?
And why do you watch wickedness?
Destruction and violence are in front of me.
Quarrels and disputes arise.
That is why your teaching is numbed,
    and justice is never carried out.
    Wicked people surround righteous people
        so that when justice is carried out, it's perverted.

In this prayer Habakkuk asks God why he allows evil to triumph. The prophet was concerned that many good people were suffering because of the wrongdoing that was allowed to take place in his society. His prayer also points out another consequence of God's inaction: God's word, his teachings to his people, is ignored. Apparently, few people in Judah were inclined to live according to God's teachings because evil was going to win anyway. Why bother to be good?

Habakkuk got an answer to his prayer. God revealed to him that the Babylonians would be his instrument to punish the evil that the people of Judah were doing (Habakkuk 1:6-7). But this raised another problem for Habakkuk. Weren't the Babylonians committing their own kind of evil? So Habakkuk prayed a second prayer:

34

Didn't you exist before time began, O LORD, my God,
    my Holy One?
 We will not die!
O LORD, you have appointed the Babylonians
    to bring judgment.
O Rock, you have destined them to correct us.
Your eyes are too pure to look at evil.
You can't watch wickedness.
  Why do you keep watching treacherous people?
  Why are you silent when wicked people swallow those
    who are more righteous than they are?
You make all people like the fish in the sea,
  like schools of sea life that have no ruler.
The Babylonians pull them all up with fishhooks,
    drag them away in nets,
       and gather them in dragnets.
          So they rejoice and are happy.
That is why they sacrifice to their nets and burn incense
  to their dragnets.
 They are rich and well fed because of them.
Will they keep on emptying their nets
  and always kill nations without mercy?

                     (Habakkuk 1:12-17)

The answer the prophet received did not solve his problem. He still thought evil would triumph over good in the world, but in a different way. If anything, it made it worse. Habakkuk knows that God cannot even look at evil. How could God use one evil to punish another? The Babylonians were an even worse evil according to Habakkuk. They were conquerors who had no mercy on people. They were idolaters who did terrible things to people who were more righteous than they. Now God was going to use them to punish the evil people in Judah. To Habakkuk this didn't seem like much of a solution to the problem of evil, and he told God as much in this second prayer.

The answer Habakkuk received reaffirmed God's decision to use Babylon to punish the evil in Judah. The prophet reported:

> Then the LORD answered me,
> "Write the vision.
>> Make it clear on tablets
>>> so that anyone can read it quickly.
> The vision will still happen at the appointed time.
>> It hurries toward its goal.
>> It won't be a lie.
> If it's delayed, wait for it.
>> It will certainly happen.
>> It won't be late."

> (Habakkuk 2:2-3)

God then continues by promising the prophet that he will punish evil people: those who are arrogant (2:4-6a), those who get rich by dishonest means (2:6b-8), those who use violence to get what they want (2:9-11), those who gain political strength through criminal activity (2:12-14), those who involve others in their wicked acts and bring God's anger on them (2:15-17), and those who worship idols (2:19). God will see that all of them are punished in some way. Therefore, the wicked Babylonians will also be punished, even though God will use them to punish others.

What was the conclusion for the prophet? "The LORD is in his holy temple. All the earth should be silent in his presence" (Habakkuk 2:20). Habakkuk realized that God is holy and therefore, cannot tolerate evil. He remains holy and from his holy temple he deals with evil. No one on earth can question his solution to the problem of evil.

We have come to the first lesson to be learned about praying to God to punish evil: *It is not wrong to ask God to deal with evil, even to punish evil people. It is wrong, however, to expect God to make the result be one in which humans can see that good unambiguously triumphs over evil.* The problem of evil in this world is much more complicated than we humans can comprehend. It runs deep within every culture. Everything in our culture that we value as good is complicated by the evil that lies deep within humans (see Romans 3:9-19). Considering the pervasive nature of evil and how closely it is tied to everything we humans do, we really cannot expect a simple "good will triumph in the end" answer to our prayers about evil. We can only trust that God does deal with evil. He alone comprehends the widespread web of evil in the world.

God's answer to our prayer may not even be recognized when it happens. Would Habakkuk have recognized the answer to his prayer about the evil in Judah if God had not revealed it to him? His reaction indicates that he would not have recognized it. And it is perhaps even more difficult for us today to recognize the answer to our prayers that God would punish evil. We want quick, simple, and straightforward solutions to all our problems. For instance, when politicians campaign for office they often offer simple, sound-bite solutions to the problems and issues of the day. We often vote on complicated issues that have been reduced to simplistic slogans. We don't demand more details of our politicians nor do we demand of ourselves detailed studies of the issues so that we can confront candidates when they dodge difficult issues with trite rhetoric. We don't want to hear anything about complicated problems. We want simple solutions.

Another sign of our attitude can be seen in the way our media reports the problems in our society. It is not unusual to see an hour-long news magazine program on television devote twenty minutes to a story that points out a problem in society or a wrong that has been done. For years now many news stories have focused on how money corrupts the political process in the United States. The stories report the tremendous amounts of money spent on campaigns and call for reforms so that those who give the money do not unfairly influence the drafting of new laws or the formulation of government policies. Some even report on a number of laws that have been passed to limit the buying of influence. Yet, the stories of the influence obtained by large donors to political candidates and parties continue to be a part of every election year, and the supposed solutions that are written into the law don't seem to stem the tide of funds streaming into the political process.

Yet, do we really believe that such a story does any more than scratch the surface of the problem? Is it the fault of the media that when a television or radio program devotes a mere hour to one story it is considered in-depth coverage? Or is it our fault because we seldom have the patience to grasp how evil has complicated our world? We don't want to take the time to understand the real root of the problem, much less the time it would take to come to a good and comprehensive solution.

It is no wonder, then, that we often cannot discern when God answers our prayers and deals with evil and evil people. His solutions deal with the intricacies and complications of life. He offers the right solution that is best for us. His answer comes. We often cannot comprehend it.

However, Habakkuk learned that God's answer to his prayer about evil was to be accepted. Chapter 3 of his prophecy records his prayer that accepts God's solutions to the presence of evil in the world. He begins by praying:

38

Lord, I have heard the report about you.
Lord, I fear your work.
  In the course of the years, renew it.
  In the course of the years, reveal it.
  In all this chaos, remember to be merciful.

(Habakkuk 3:2)

Throughout this prayer Habakkuk displays a healthy fear and respect for God's power to act against evil. He now knows that sometimes the people or things God uses to punish evil in this world are powerful. He knows that such power can bring suffering. Yet, he prays God will continue to do his work and to renew it as the years run their course. He also prays God will reveal his work so it can be seen and appreciated. But most of all, he prays God will remember to be merciful. When God used the Babylonians to punish evil, Habakkuk saw that many people would suffer. He prays God would remember to be merciful so the suffering is limited by God's mercy. Habakkuk came to respect God's power. His prayer is now more mature. He wants God to use his power to punish wickedness. At the same time, he recognizes God could punish all people for their failings. So he now prays God would remember to be merciful. He teaches us that when we pray for God to reverse evil's triumph over good, we must also ask God to temper his anger with mercy so that we do not all perish. When our prayer for God to deal with evil in the world or specific evils that touch our lives becomes a mature prayer, we will be able to pray as Habakkuk did:

  Even if the fig tree does not bloom
    and the vines have no grapes,
  even if the olive tree fails to produce
    and the fields yield no food,
  even if the sheep pen is empty

and the stalls have no cattle—
even then,
    I will be happy with the Lord.
    I will truly find joy in God, who saves me.
    The Lord Almighty is my strength.
      He makes my feet like those of a deer.
      He makes me walk on the mountains.

(Habakkuk 3:17-19)

## Nehemiah and the Apostles: Praying for Blessing When Beset by Evil

Is calling on God to punish evil the only attitude we should adopt when we pray? Or do alternatives to the type of prayers prayed by the Judeans in Babylon by Jeremiah and by Habakkuk exist? At least two alternatives exist. One is found in the book of Nehemiah. Nehemiah not only prayed that God would remember those who did evil things (Nehemiah 6:14, 13:29), he also prayed that God would remember the good that he did:

> Remember me, my God. Consider everything that I have done for these people.
>
> (Nehemiah 5:19)

> "Remember me for what I have done, my God, and don't wipe out the good things that I have done for your temple and for the worship that is held there."
>
> (Nehemiah 13:14)

> "Remember me also for this, my God, and spare me, since you are very kind."
>
> (Nehemiah 13:22b)

> "Remember me, my God, for my benefit."
>
> (Nehemiah 13:31b)

Nehemiah did pray God would punish the evil actions of those who opposed his work for God's people or who disregarded God's word and the welfare of his people. But these prayers show that his primary response to evil's seeming triumph in the world was to ask God to bless him and his work. He focused his prayers against evil on the good God could accomplish through him. Instead of merely praying God would punish evil, he prayed God would reward good. This is another way of confronting triumphant evil in the world. Nehemiah confronted evil through action. He prayed God would bless him for the good he did and would allow it to flourish.

Here we have a second lesson about praying when evil seems to be winning: *Our prayers can be proactive. They can ask God for blessings and for good to come from what we do.* In this way our prayers can be answered as God moves us to action. Instead of being immobilized by evil that appears to dominate, we can pray God will bless us and our actions as forces for good. Nehemiah was not stopped from doing good because he was opposed by some very powerful men who intended to use their power to harm his people. Instead, he prayed God would continue to make him an agent that would accomplish something beneficial for others.

The rage we feel when evil triumphs over good can paralyze us. Nehemiah's prayers show us that there is an alternative to that paralysis. The alternative is to pray that God would move us to do what is right and beneficial for others. Pray that God would bless us and reverse the effects of evil in our lives. Such prayers are not self-centered. Rather, they are prayers that teach us how to combat evil in the world by using the blessings God gives us.

The apostles prayed the same type of prayer when the authorities in Jerusalem threatened them. They prayed:

"Master, you made the sky, the land, the sea, and everything in them. You said through the Holy Spirit, who spoke through your servant David (our ancestor),

> 'Why do the nations act arrogantly?
> Why do their people devise useless plots?
>> Kings take their stand.
>> Rulers make plans together
>>> against the Lord and against his Messiah.'

"In this city Herod and Pontius Pilate made plans together with non-Jewish people and the people of Israel. They made their plans against your holy servant Jesus, whom you anointed. Through your will and power, they did everything that you had already decided should be done.

"Lord, pay attention to their threats now, and allow us to speak your word boldly. Show your power by healing, performing miracles, and doing amazing things through the power and the name of your holy servant Jesus."

(Acts 4:24-30)

Instead of being paralyzed by inaction and praying for God to punish the authorities, they prayed God would use them to accomplish good and overcome the evil the authorities had in mind. Such prayers are prayers of faith and trust that God can use us, even when we are most oppressed by the evil done by others.

# Stephen:
## Praying for Those Who Do Evil

A third possible response to evil is found in Acts 7:59-60:

> While council members were executing Stephen, he called out, "Lord Jesus, welcome my spirit." Then he knelt down and shouted, "Lord, don't hold this sin against them." After he had said this, he died.

Stephen's prayer is perhaps the hardest response to evil. It is easy to angrily ask God to punish those who commit crimes. It is not uncommon to see relatives of someone murdered calling for the punishment and even execution of those who are accused of committing the murder. Stephen's prayer asks God to overlook the sins of those who were murdering him. How can we find the compassion in our hearts to pray like that? Where can we find the resources to ask God to overlook or forgive the willfully wicked acts of people who simply don't care whether they are evil?

Perhaps it would be easier to pray Jesus' prayer from the cross, "'Father, forgive them. They don't know what they're doing'" (Luke 23:34). We could possibly find a way to pray for those who commit some evil act against us if we thought that they did not realize the gravity of what they were doing. But in Stephen's case, his killers knew what they were doing. They refused to listen to what Stephen had to say and were intent on killing him (Acts 7:57). Yet, even then, Stephen asked God not to hold their sin against them. Such prayers take human compassion beyond what we expect of even the best people.

The key to being able to pray this type of prayer in the face of cruelest evil is found in what Stephen saw while he was being killed. Luke tells us that Stephen saw God's glory in heaven and

Jesus standing in the position of authority on God's right side (Acts 7:55). As we saw in the previous chapter, prayer is intended to focus us on God. Stephen was focused on God and saw his glory. That glory was associated with Jesus, who brought forgiveness to everyone and who is in heaven, ruling with all authority. Stephen could pray for the pardon of his killers because he understood he had God's forgiveness. He saw the glory of God in pardoning sinners through the death of Jesus. And he saw that Jesus was in control of all things. He could leave the punishment for his death in Jesus' hands. He could concentrate on the glory of God that we all can see in the forgiveness God offers us. As we focus our prayer on God, we can also find the compassion to pray for those who do many of the terrible evil acts in the world.

The Bible contains many prayers about the problem of evil, and all of them are worth studying. You may also want to read Moses' prayer to God in Numbers 11:10-15 as another example of prayer in response to wickedness. Many of the psalms address this problem as one of their major themes.[1] When evil seems to be winning and you are outraged at the immorality of others that has hurt you, a good way to handle your feelings and emotions is by contemplating on one of these prayers. Then pray and focus on God who alone can conquer evil.

# 3

# *When Sin Is Recognized*

UILT IS A powerful emotion. It can cause us to alter our behavior. Some people feel so guilty about something they have done, they will go out of their way to avoid situations in which they may have to face the persons they have harmed. Others go out of their way to be nice to those whom they hurt. A child may be especially nice to a parent, or a spouse may buy a special gift for their partner because of guilt.

I once knew a man who headed a small organization. He had one serious flaw: he was jealous when those under him succeeded. He didn't want to share any credit with them and felt as if he were being kept out of the spotlight when they were praised for their work. As a way of keeping them from outshining his performance, often he would deny them opportunities to work on projects they would have found rewarding. When they proposed ideas to solve problems or when they offered insights that could have kept the organization from making costly errors, he would ignore them, berate their ideas, rate them poorly on their annual evaluations after they had accomplished much, or shuffle them off to another position (even demote them or fire them). This way he would not have to share the glory with others or admit that his decisions had perhaps caused the problems to begin with.

Needless to say, this was not good for morale, nor was it good for the supervisor's conscience. He would try to win back the employees favor by buying them lunch or with a promise of some perk, promises that often went unfulfilled. At other times he would try to give them pep talks and tell them what great accomplishments they were achieving, all the while implying that he was the main reason that they were accomplishing anything, even when he had made the mistakes. Sometimes the pep talks would turn into ways of defending the organization's failed policies, often set by the supervisor himself. The pep talks could even transform themselves into opportunities for reminding the employees of their unspeakable sin of trying to offer suggestions for improvements.

But this behavior did not win back the employee's favor and boost morale because it was merely a way of covering up his guilt, and the employees knew it. Instead of having the effect he intended, his behavior deepened his feelings of guilt and further alienated the workers. His temporary change in behavior was no substitute for facing his guilt and admitting that he had harmed others to satisfy his own ego.

Behavior is not the only thing that can change when someone is feeling guilty. Our attitude can change. Like the supervisor's bad performance evaluations of his employees, we can blame the people whom we harmed and attempt to convince ourselves it was their fault, not ours. If that does not seem to be a good avenue to escape our guilt, we can deny what we did. We can deny our guilt even to the point where we convince ourselves that we did not do what we actually did. In extreme cases some people have become pathological liars because of guilt. They deny the truth so easily that they believe their own lies. In less extreme cases people engage in a personal revision of history, redefining their actions in ways that convince them that what they have done was harmless or even beneficial for others, like the supervisor's self-serving pep talks.

Another strategy people use to cope with guilt is redefining what is right and wrong, as the supervisor did in his defensive pep talks. This is done by equating what is legally allowable with what is ethically and morally right. At other times people simply deny that there can be any absolute moral code by which we should all live. Personal opinion on right and wrong is all that matters. Guilt is gone because no standard can be used to make us feel guilty.

Of course, all of these ways of coping with guilt create more problems than they solve. If we are nice to someone because we feel guilty, they may resent us even more. They may want us to be nice to them out of sincere feelings toward them and not because we are trying to work ourselves into their good graces. Or they may take advantage of our guilt and use it to get what they want. In either case we do not get what we are really trying to obtain—a renewed relationship. If we resort to changing our attitude and blaming others or denying to ourselves what we have done, we develop very unhealthy behavior. That behavior could lead us to make more mistakes in the future and even into self-destructive behavior. If we hide behind the law or behind an attitude that no objective standard of behavior can govern our lives, we can hardly complain when others harm us. When we choose one of these ways of coping with guilt, we choose to avoid solving our problem.

The Bible, however, offers us a real solution to the problem of guilt. Instead of trying to cope with it, we can follow the example of biblical prayers and recognize our guilt and admit we were wrong. For many people this is the most difficult way to deal with it. The mechanisms we have for handling guilt are ways of trying to save ourselves the embarrassment and uncomfortable feelings that come with admitting we have done something that is morally or ethically wrong. We want to escape the feeling that we have harmed someone. Although our ways of coping with guilt may seem like an escape, they may cause more complications for our lives. The Bible's solution, though uncomfortable, solves the problem of guilt.

As we examine some prayers in the Bible that were spoken by people who admitted their wrongs and recognized their guilt, we will discover three important truths:

1. Prayers of confession should not be prayed as an easy way out of our guilt nor as a way to escape the negative consequences of sin. Prayers of confession should be prayed because we trust God's promise of forgiveness.

2. True prayers of confession are also prayers of repentance. That is, true confession is not only admitting we have sinned, but also it is a willingness to change our attitude and actions.

3. Because of our sin we do not deserve to stand before God and ask for his forgiveness. The Bible's prayers of confession recognize that because of our faults and errors we do not deserve God's forgiveness. Prayers of confession cannot demand forgiveness because of who we are or what we have done, but they can give us confidence that God will forgive because of who God is.

# Psalms 32 and 130:
## Personal Prayers for Forgiveness

One example of a prayer from someone who recognized sin and admitted his sinfulness to God is Psalm 32:

Blessed is the person whose disobedience is forgiven
and whose sin is pardoned.
Blessed is the person whom the LORD never accuses of sin
and who has no deceitful thoughts.

When I kept silent ⌊about my sins⌋,
my bones began to weaken because of my groaning
all day long.
Day and night your hand laid heavily on me.
My strength shriveled in the summer heat.           *Selah*

I made my sins known to you, and I did not cover up my guilt.
I decided to confess them to you, O LORD.
Then you forgave all my sins.           *Selah*

For this reason let all godly people pray to you
when you may be found.
Then raging floodwater will not reach them.

You are my hiding place.
You protect me from trouble.
You surround me with joyous songs of salvation.           *Selah*

⌊The LORD says,⌋
"I will instruct you.
I will teach you the way that you should go.
I will advise you as my eyes watch over you.
Don't be stubborn like a horse or mule.
⌊They need⌋ a bit and bridle in their mouth to restrain them,
or they will not come near you."

Many heartaches await wicked people,
  but mercy surrounds those who trust the LORD.

Be glad and find joy in the LORD, you righteous people.
  Sing with joy, all whose motives are decent.

This psalm, along with Psalms 6, 38, 51, 102, 130, and 143, is one of the seven penitential psalms. Since ancient times the Christian church has used these psalms on special days set aside for us to confess sin and admit to God that we have not lived according to his law. The church recognized that the proper way to deal with guilt is confession. These seven psalms are examples of how to pray to God when we recognize that we have sinned.

Psalm 32 is a typical psalm of confession. The psalmist begins by reminding himself of the blessings of forgiveness and pardon. The Lord no longer accuses those whom he has forgiven, and those people have stopped deceiving themselves about their sinful actions. That blessing is what drew the psalmist to prayer. He may have felt uncomfortable confessing his sins. He may have felt that he would lose face in front of others by admitting he was wrong, but he valued God's forgiveness and the blessings it brings more than he feared the consequences of admitting his sin.

He had already experienced the consequences of hiding his sin. It affected him not only spiritually and emotionally, but also physically. He groaned, he felt his guilt in his bones, and he lost his strength. Many physicians and psychologists recognize that physical ailments can have spiritual and psychological causes. The psalmist knew that long ago. Other psalms speak of the same thing:

O LORD, do not punish me in your anger
  or discipline me in your rage.

Have pity on me, O LORD, because I am weak.
Heal me, O LORD, because my bones shake with terror.
My soul has been deeply shaken with terror.
(Psalm 6:1-3a)

My guilt has overwhelmed me.
Like a heavy load, it is more than I can bear.
My wounds smell rotten.
They fester because of my stupidity.
I am bent over and bowed down very low.
All day I walk around in mourning.
My insides are filled with burning pain,
and no healthy spot is left on my body.
I am numb and completely devastated.
I roar because my heart's in turmoil.
You know all my desires, O Lord,
and my groaning has not been hidden from you.
My heart is pounding.
I have lost my strength.
Even the light of my eyes has left me.
(Psalm 38:4-10)

Guilt showed itself through psychological and physical ailments in the lives of these psalmists. They had tried to cope with their guilt, but its effects on their lives made it unbearable. Yet, what really motivated them to admit their wrongs and pray for forgiveness was not the negative consequences of their feelings of guilt, but the positive blessings promised by God. Those blessings are what the psalmist first mentioned in his prayer, and they were the focus of his plea to God.

Thus, the first lesson we learn from Psalm 32 is very important: *Prayers of confession should not be prayed as an easy way out of our guilt nor as a way to escape the negative consequences of sin.*

*Prayers of confession should be prayed because we trust God's promise of forgiveness.* For the psalmist, confessing his sin was not merely saying he had sinned. It was not a quick and easy way to escape his sin. It was not a psychological game to clear his conscience. Rather, it was a prayer of trust in God.

The psalmist acknowledged that God answered his prayer: "I made my sins known to you, and I did not cover up my guilt. I decided to confess them to you, O LORD. Then you forgave all my sins" (Psalm 32:5). The psalmist does not tell us how he received God's forgiveness. Perhaps, in keeping with Old Testament practices, he went to the temple, confessed his sins, offered a sacrifice, and received forgiveness through the priest. But whatever way he received forgiveness from God, it changed his life in three ways.

First, the psalmist's attitude toward God changed. He developed a closer relationship with his Lord. He called God his hiding place. He looked to God for protection. He found comfort in knowing that God surrounded him with the joy that comes in knowing that God had saved him from his sin and guilt. That joy freed him from the need to sin. Often we sin because we aren't comfortable with God's ways of doing things. We do not trust that God is completely in control of everything in life, so we attempt to do things our way. We take shortcuts around God's law and try to make our lives better because of our selfish, self-centered impulses. Often we sin because we try to gain something for ourselves or avoid losing something that we have. We do not trust that if we follow God's way of doing things, God will provide all we need. The psalmist's life changed because he was now willing to trust God instead of his own self-centered impulse.

Often, parents try to counter God's way of accomplishing things in their children's life. As parents, we want the best for our children, and we want to spare them the pain that comes from failure. The parent who automatically blames a teacher when his child is having problems in school can actually be working against God's will. If the problem is the student's, the best thing that can be done is to help the child face the problem and learn to rise above it. But instead of allowing God to work through failure and being an aid to a son or daughter's growth, some parents allow their children to escape the challenge to learn by blaming the teacher or the school. Every teacher who has taught at any level from kindergarten through college has witnessed this tragedy of parents who try to spare their children from failure, only to make matters worse. They also know that parents who accept the challenges God puts before their children and who help them learn from them turn the challenges into a positive just as the psalmist did.

Second, his attitude toward receiving guidance from God changed. He now recognized that instead of organizing his life according to his desires, he could learn from God. When he sinned he was being stubborn like a mule that needs to have a bit and bridle to guide it. Now that he had received forgiveness, he was willing to learn from God and ordered his life according to God's instruction, trusting that God would watch over him.

Third, he now wanted to tell others of the benefits of trusting God. He didn't keep the relationship he had with God a secret, but he wanted others to enjoy that relationship. Therefore, the end of his prayer does not speak to God, but to others. It shows us the benefits of trusting in God and receiving his mercy. It urges us to offer prayers of confession.

Recently, I have had the privilege of serving a congregation as interim pastor while they search for a new pastor. In this congregation there is a remarkable phenomenon. Though I am able to serve only part time and not able to do all the things that a full-time, permanent pastor would do, the congregation continues to add new members. The reason for this is not because I am leading an evangelism effort for the congregation (which I don't have the time to do). Instead, it is because members of the congregation tell others about their relationship with God. They have experienced the change in their relationship with God because they have received forgiveness from him. Therefore, they naturally share that joy with others, and this brings new members to the church. These Christians have found what the psalmist found, and they tell others about it.

These changes in the psalmist's life that we find in his prayer lead to a second conclusion about prayers of confession: *True prayers of confession are also prayers of repentance.* That is, true confession is not only admitting we have sinned, but also it is a willingness to change our attitude and actions. The psalmist did not believe in a cheap confession that admitted his wrongdoing but then did nothing about it. He believed that true confession involved a willingness to change his life. This willingness came from the forgiveness and mercy he received from God. Because of his new relationship with God based on God's mercy, he wanted to change. Receiving true forgiveness from God brought him into a relationship that he wanted to have with his Lord permanently. This meant he wanted to change his attitude toward God's law and his behavior towards others. Recognizing sin is the first step in going to God in prayer and confessing our sin. But other steps are involved in prayers that confess our sins. The outcome of all those steps is a changed attitude due to our new relationship with God.

Notice that the same concerns are found in another prayer of confession in the Bible, Psalm 130:

O Lord, out of the depths I call to you.
O Lord, hear my voice.
Let your ears be open to my pleas for mercy.
O Lord, who would be able to stand
 if you kept a record of sins?
But with you there is forgiveness
 so that you can be feared.
I wait for the Lord, my soul waits,
 and with hope I wait for his word.
My soul waits for the Lord
 more than those who watch for the morning,
 more than those who watch for the morning.
O Israel, put your hope in the Lord,
 because with the Lord there is mercy
  and with him there is unlimited forgiveness.
  He will rescue Israel from all its sins.

This psalm expresses the same concerns as Psalm 32. It is a confession of sin based on God's mercy, and it shows the psalmist's changed attitude as a result of God's mercy. Yet this psalm highlights another basic truth about biblical prayers of confession. The psalmist asks the rhetorical question, "O Lord, who would be able to stand if you kept a record of sins?" The answer to this question is "No one." As the next line in the prayer states, it is only God's forgiveness that allows us to continue living. This psalm teaches us another truth about prayers of confession: *Because of our sin we do not deserve to stand before God and ask for his forgiveness.* The Bible's prayers of confession recognize that because of our faults and errors we do not deserve God's forgiveness. Prayers of confession cannot demand forgiveness because of who we are or what we have done. But prayers for forgiveness can be confident that God will forgive because of who God is. He has unlimited forgiveness, as the psalmist tells us. Prayers of confession, like all other prayers, focus on God and not on the person who is praying.

## Ezra's Group Prayer for Forgiveness

The Bible also contains prayers of confession prayed by groups. When Ezra was informed that his people had disobeyed God's law, he prayed in front of God's temple where he was joined by many others (Ezra 10:1). His prayer is recorded in Ezra 9:6-15:

"I am ashamed, my God. I am embarrassed to look at you. Our sins have piled up over our heads, and our guilt is so overwhelming that it reaches heaven. From our ancestors' days until now, we have been deep in guilt. Our kings and our priests have been handed over to foreign kings to be executed. We have been taken captive, robbed, and humiliated, as we still are today because of our sins. And now, for a brief moment, the LORD our God has been kind enough to leave us a few survivors from Babylon and to give us a secure hold on his holy place. Our God has made our eyes light up and has given us new opportunities while we were slaves. We are slaves, but our God hasn't abandoned us in our slavery. Instead, he has made the kings of Persia treat us kindly. He did this to give us an opportunity to rebuild our God's temple and restore its ruins and to give us a protective wall in Judah and Jerusalem.

"And now, our God, what can we say after all this? We have abandoned your commandments! The commandments you gave us through your servants the prophets, said, 'The land you are going to take possession of has been polluted by its perverted people and by their disgusting practices that have filled it with wickedness from one end to another. So never let your daughters marry their sons or your sons marry their daughters, and never seek peace or trade with them. Then you will be strong, be able to eat the good things the land produces, and be able to give this land as a long-lasting inheritance to your children.'

"After all that has happened to us because of the evil things we have done and because of our overwhelming guilt, you, our God, have punished us far less than we deserve and have permitted a few of us to survive. If we break your commandments again and intermarry with people doing these disgusting things, you will become even more angry with us until you finally destroy us and no survivors are left. Lord God of Israel, because you are fair, a few of us continue to remain as survivors. Look at us. All of us are guilty. None of us can stand in your presence because of this."

This prayer started as a personal prayer prayed in a public place. It soon became a public prayer. Ezra's confession is an interesting one. He notes "From our ancestors' days until now, we have been deep in guilt." He confesses that not only he and his people in his day had sinned, but also his ancestors had sinned. Is he claiming that he is guilty because of the sins of his ancestors? No, rather he notes that one of the sins he and his people have is that they did not learn from the sins of their ancestors. God punished the kings and priests that went before them for not obeying his commands. Now they, also, had disobeyed God's commands to them.

Moreover, their sin was worse. God gave them new opportunities. They were permitted to return to the land their ancestors lost. However, they repeated the sins that cost their ancestors the land. But despite all of that, Ezra prayed and confessed the sins of his people. Although he did not directly ask for God's forgiveness, his prayer clearly relies on God's promise to forgive those who confess their sin, even though they had repeatedly ignored God's command to them.

One interesting aspect of this prayer is that the sin confessed is one that Ezra was not personally guilty of committing. His prayer revolves around one command that God gave to his ancient people—not to intermarry wiith the idolatrous people of Canaan (see Exodus 34:12-16). Ezra had not done this, but he confesses this sin because a number of his people had. Perhaps he assumed that he was partially responsible because he had not spoken out against the marriages in time to prevent the people from entering into marriages that God had forbidden. However, even if that was not his motivation, he recognized he was part of a society that was ignoring God's commands, and he needed to confess the sins of his people, including himself.

We can use this as a guide for prayers of confession today. Many Christians decry the evils that they see in society. Christians even seek to use political means to change laws that they understand to be immoral. None of that is wrong in itself, but how often do we pray to God about the sins of our society and plead for forgiveness? Even if we have not taken part in the particular immoral or unethical aspects of our society, shouldn't we, like Ezra, confess those sins?

We need to confess the sins of our society because we are part of it. No matter which culture Christians are a part of, they are affected by it. The solutions to our countries' problems are not solved by Christians self-righteously viewing ourselves completely separate from our culture and unaffected by its sins. If Ezra had done that, he would have created a distance between himself and the people who were disobeying God's command. By remaining a part of a society that was ignoring God's command, he was able to pray a prayer that transformed his nation. His prayer was a request for forgiveness that would touch the lives of every one of his people so they all would change.

We ought to pray prayers of confession about our countries' ills, including confessing our role in the evils that afflict our society and its people. Christians are always a part of a larger community. At times we take part in the practices and assumptions that are common to our culture, not realizing that they may be at odds with God's will. Prayers of corporate confession prayed publicly in church or privately at home are a beginning in the fight to overcome the ills of our culture.

## Daniel's Private Prayer
## for Mercy Toward an Entire People

The Bible records two private prayers of corporate confession. The first is Daniel 9:4-19. There Daniel tells us:

> I prayed to the LORD my God. I confessed and said, "Lord, you are great and deserve respect as the only God. You keep your promise and show mercy to those who love you and obey your commandments. We have sinned, done wrong, acted wickedly, rebelled, and turned away from your commandments and laws. We haven't listened to your servants the prophets, who spoke in your name to our kings, leaders, ancestors, and all the common people. You, Lord, are righteous. But we—the men of Judah, the citizens of Jerusalem, and all the Israelites whom you scattered in countries near and far—are still ashamed because we have been

unfaithful to you. We, our kings, leaders, and ancestors are ashamed because we have sinned agains you, LORD.

"But you, Lord our God, are compassionate and forgiving, although we have rebelled against you. We never listened to you or lived by the teachings you gave us through your servants the prophets. All Israel has ignored your teachings and refused to listen to you. So you brought on us the curses you swore in an oath, the curses written in the Teachings of your servant Moses. We sinned against you. So you did what you said you would do to us and our rulers by bringing a great disaster on us. Nowhere in the world has anything ever happened like what has happened to Jerusalem. This entire disaster happened to us, exactly as it was written in Moses' Teachings. LORD our God, we never tried to gain your favor by turning from our wrongs and dedicating ourselves to your truth. So you were prepared to bring this disaster on us. LORD our God, you are righteous in everything you do. But we never listened to you.

"Lord our God, you brought your people out of Egypt with your strong hand and made yourself famous even today. We have sinned and done evil things. Lord, since you are very righteous, turn your anger and fury away from your city, Jerusalem, your holy mountain. Jerusalem and your people are insulted by everyone around us because of our sins and the wicked things our ancestors did.

"Our God, listen to my prayer and request. For your own sake, Lord, look favorably on your holy place, which is lying in ruins. Open your ears and listen, my God. Open your eyes and look at our ruins and at the city called by your name. We are not requesting this from you because we are righteous, but because you are very compassionate. Listen to us, Lord. Forgive us, Lord. Pay attention, and act. Don't delay! Do this for your sake, my God, because your city and your people are called by your name."

This prayer of confession has four main parts. In the first part Daniel contrasts God's faithfulness to the unfaithfulness of Daniel's people. God's great act of faithfulness that Daniel mentions in his prayer is that God shows mercy to those who love him and obey him. Notice that Daniel admits that even those who obey God must rely on his mercy. Even if we obeyed God perfectly (and none of us have) we still would have to rely on God's mercy. Our Creator does not owe us anything. Yet he is merciful. He promised to show mercy to those who loved him and obeyed him (Exodus 20:6), and he went beyond that promise. Israel not only disobeyed God but also rebelled against him. In his mercy God sent prophets to warn his people about the consequences of their rebellion and to invite them to keep his law again. They refused, and Daniel admits this in his prayer.

The second part of his prayer contrasts God's compassion and forgiveness to his people's rejection of God's forgiveness. Note that in Daniel's prayer, acknowledgment of God's forgiveness is lived out by obeying God. The person who has truly received God's forgiveness *wants* to live the way God teaches us to live.

However, Daniel had to admit, "'We never listened to you or lived by the teachings you gave us through your servants the prophets. All Israel has ignored your teachings and refused to listen to you'"(Daniel 9:10-11). The word translated *teachings* is the Hebrew word *torah*. This word is often translated *law*. However, the

Hebrew word denotes more than the idea of laws that tell us what to do or what not to do. It is more than a way for people to rigidly determine what they should do in every situation by applying a set of laws. The root meaning of the Hebrew word *torah* is *instruction*. God instructed his people in how they were to live. They did not receive only laws. They received laws in the context of instructions to show each other love, mercy and forgiveness—the thibngs that God showed them. When they did not show these things toward others, they showed that they had rejected God's forgiveness. Daniel's prayer admits that Israel received God's punishment because they rejected God's forgiveness.

The third part of Daniel's prayer is a request. He asks God to forgive his people again. He bases his request on God's great act in the Old Testament God's forgiveness—leading the people out of Egypt. Throughout the Old Testament this one great act of God is the defining moment of Israel's relationship with the Lord. When they were totally helpless with the mightiest army in the world bearing down on them, God parted the Red Sea and saved them. They did nothing and God did everything (Exodus 14:13-14). By picking this example Daniel is again relying on God to do everything needed to grant his request.

The final section of Daniel's prayer calls on God to listen. In this section he repeats that he is relying on God and his compassion and forgiveness. He admits that the reason God should act is not because Daniel or his people are deserving but because God and his honor deserve to be recognized by all people.

# A Pattern for Penitential Prayer

### FOCUS ON GOD

Daniel's prayer combines all the lessons learned about confessing our sins in prayer. But it does more than that. It also shows us a way to organize our prayers of confession. A good way to start a prayer of confession (or any prayer for that matter) is to start with a description of God. Daniel began, "Lord, you are great and deserve respect as the only God. You keep your promise and show mercy to those who love you and obey your commandments" (Daniel 9:4). Daniel focused his prayer on God by speaking about who God is. In this case the things he said about God were appropriate to his prayer. They told God why he was praying and helped him to remain focused on the things about God that prompted his prayer.

### PRAY FOR YOUR NEED

The next thing that we can mention in our prayer is our need. In this case Daniel mentioned the need of his people by first noting what they were in contrast to God. They needed forgiveness because they were unlike God. He was faithful. They were not.

### PRAY ABOUT WHAT GOD HAS *ALREADY* DONE FOR YOU

This can be followed by focusing on what God has already done for us. In Daniel's day that was the release from slavery in Egypt. For Christians today God's defining act is the life, death, and resurrection of Jesus. In Jesus, God has freed us from the slavery to sin and death—precisely what we are praying about in our prayers of confession.

Finally, we can bring our request for forgiveness and healing to God. In this request we not only can ask for forgiveness, but also we can ask God to heal us so that we change and so the results of forgiveness show in our lives in concrete ways. Depending on what we are confessing, this may be different things at different times. However, it is an important part of our attitude toward God's forgiveness. Daniel wanted change for his people. He did not state directly what he wanted that change to be. However, by praying that God would lift his anger against Jerusalem, he was implying that his people would be changed so that they would return to Jerusalem. There they would worship God and live according to his teachings that he gave through the prophets. Today, we should also want God to change us so that his teachings through the prophets and through the apostles make a difference in the way we live.

While our prayers of confession do not have to follow this outline, it is a very useful one. It can help us focus on God and his mercy and make our prayers ones of true confession and real repentance. It is not easy for us ever to admit our guilt, even to God. Our pride does not want to admit that we are not worthy of God's mercy and compassion. Moreover, we don't want to rely on God's mercy and forgiveness given to us even though we have sinned. Admitting that draws an even sharper contrast between us and God, and we don't look good in that contrast. Yet the only way to really deal with our sins in a healthy way is to learn to pray prayers of confession such as the ones we have looked at in this chapter. God forgives our sins and mends our lives that have been broken by our own failures. When we learn that, we have to pray and confess, and we'll find it impossible to delay our prayer.

The Bible contains other prayers of confession you may want to read. Nehemiah 1:5-10 is a prayer by Nehemiah about his people's sins and his desire to help them as they rebuilt Jerusalem. In a sense it is a follow-up to Daniel's prayer and is similar to it. You may also want to look at a few psalms of confession, especially Psalms 15, 52, and 79 as well as three of the seven penitential psalms not treated in this chapter: Psalms 51, 102, and 143.

*4*

# When Health Fails

EALTH AND FITNESS have become an obsession for many in the United States. News programs on radio and television regularly feature items on health, fitness, and medicine. Many newspapers have weekly sections devoted to health issues. We receive constant advice on diet, exercise, and ways to prevent disease. We hear of new medical procedures and treatments, and we are aware of how much this has increased our expected life spans.

None of this, however, seems to have stopped us from worries about our health. No matter how good our medical knowledge has become, we are still subject to infirmities due to the spread of disease, our environment, and the inevitable process of aging. Knowing more about the causes of disease as well as its prevention and treatment has not meant that we are immune from the threat of disease. We can spend thousands of dollars or even an entire life's savings on treating ill health, but we cannot escape disease, sickness, or death.

It is not as if we don't try to escape ill health. Access to health care has become an important issue for public policy in the United States. Those who don't have health insurance desperately want it, or they want access to treatment through a government program. Those who do have health insurance are at times reluctant to leave one job for another because they are afraid their new company's health insurance may not cover them or their family. Systems of national health insurance have been proposed, but they have not been adopted because of fears that a new system will be too expensive, or the care will not be as good.

Why all this fear of ill health? Part of our fear is a quality of life issue. We know that chronic ill health can mean our lives are complicated by physical limitations, pain, and loss of income. Part of our anxiety is fear of death. Ill health can be a prelude to death. In fact, for most of human history when a person was so sick that they could not get out of bed, people assumed death was near. We seldom speak of someone being on their deathbed today, but the fear of sickness leading to death remains.

However, there is a reason that our society has such an obsession with avoiding ill health. Spiritual poverty leads us to desperateness when we face our mortality. Often, we cling to physical health so tightly because we have a real lack of spiritual health. In our contemporary world view we have often divorced our physical and spiritual lives from one another. Instead of using a time of sickness or ill health as a reflection on our well-being from all perspectives, we often moan and complain about our physical state and neglect our spiritual side. Some are so spiritually impoverished that when a loved one is near death, they will urge physicians to do every possible treatment for them. They do this even though the physicians may have advised them that little or no hope exists for successful treatment. Instead of turning to spiritual resources, we are tempted to turn to highly advanced medical procedures or even experimental and non-conventional treatments to save us.

What do the prayers in the Bible teach us about dealing with failing health? Can we find in the prayers of the Scriptures a way to achieve a proper balance between physical and spiritual needs in time of our sickness? We find this balance when we learn two important lessons that the prayers we will examine in the chapter teach us:

1. Trust in God leads to prayers that are able to bring all our concerns, pains, frustrations, and worries openly to God.
2. Our God is greater than everything in this life. He will outlast our life and our world. During poor or failing health we can praise God because we know he will have compassion on us no matter what the outcome of our disease.

## Hezekiah's Prayer for Healing

A variety of approaches to the problems of failing health are evident in biblical prayers. One of them is presented in the prayer by King Hezekiah when he was told by the prophet Isaiah that he was dying. He prayed, "'Please, LORD, remember how I've lived faithfully and sincerely in your presence. I've done what you consider right'" (2 Kings 20:3; Isaiah 38:3).

In this short prayer Hezekiah pointed out he had not only done what God considered the right thing to do but also he had done it sincerely. Hezekiah reformed Israel's worship. He campaigned to rid Israel of idolatry. He was faithful to the Lord in the face of the most powerful army of his day, the Assyrians. All of this was unusual for the kings of Judah. Very few of the kings had been as faithful to the Lord as Hezekiah had. His zeal for God is told to us not only in the book of Kings, but also is noted in Isaiah and hinted at in Proverbs (see Proverbs 25:1). Hezekiah appeals to this love for the Lord in his prayer.

However, Hezekiah's prayer does not imply that God owes him a favor because of the faithfulness he had shown throughout his life. He begins his prayer with "please." This word occurs only thirteen times in the Hebrew Bible. It is a special word for a sincere request, never a demand or expectation. Hezekiah recognized that God did not have to allow him to live. His faith was not going to fail if God allowed him to die. Yet, Hezekiah does remind God of his exemplary life. He asks God to take his life into account.

In Hezekiah's case God not only heard the prayer but also granted his request. Hezekiah lived for fifteen more years. God granted Hezekiah, one of the most faithful kings of Judah, longer life. Isaiah records for us Hezekiah's prayer of thanks to God for the gift of health and a longer life (Isaiah 38:9-20).

But that is not all we learn about Hezekiah's reaction to God's gift. Unfortunately, Hezekiah did not use his gift of health properly. In 2 Kings, Isaiah, and 2 Chronicles, we read about Hezekiah's foolish pride when ambassadors from Babylon came to visit him. In 2 Chronicles 32:25-26 it says:

> But Hezekiah was conceited, so he didn't repay the LORD for his kindness. The LORD became angry with him, with Judah, and with Jerusalem. Hezekiah and the people living in Jerusalem humbled themselves when they realized they had become conceited. So the LORD didn't vent his anger on them during Hezekiah's time.

Here we learn two things about God's answer to Hezekiah's prayer. First, we see that God's original intention that Hezekiah die may have been better, but God nevertheless granted Hezekiah's request. Second, we learn that Hezekiah allowed God's answer to become a temptation. He became conceited, and this self-centered attitude led him to neglect his devotion to God. Fortunately, Hezekiah, despite his conceit, remained a man of God. When he recognized his sin, he and his people confessed their sins. Instead of remaining conceited, they learned once again that humans cannot claim any special status before God because of who they are or what they have done.

We can learn some valuable lessons from Hezekiah's prayer. First, we can learn that while human physical frailties are difficult for us to accept when they strike us, they can be what is best for us. While we may pray to be released from the effects of sickness or injury, God may know that we can serve him better or be better off with our limitations. Hezekiah became conceited when he was allowed by God to overcome the physical limitations of death. We also can be tempted to think of ourselves too highly when we enjoy good health that allows us to live lives without the humbling effect that sickness or injury might bring. This same lesson was taught to the Apostle Paul when he prayed to God and asked for improved health. God reminded Paul that his physical weakness allowed Paul to trust God's strength (2 Corinthians 12:7-10).

Many today are obsessed with maintaining not only good health, but youthfulness. Many products are sold on the appeal that they will make us appear younger or feel younger. We want to reverse the effects of aging. Aging brings on physical limitations. Most forty-year-old people cannot do everything they did at twenty. Our bodies slow down. We have small aches and pains. At fifty or sixty or seventy we cannot expect to be as physically active as we were when we were younger. Many people spend money on exercise machines in a vain attempt to remain youthful. If the intent is to stay as physically fit as God will allow us, exercise and fitness are good things. Is our pursuit of youthfulness an unspoken prayer to God to reverse what he has determined to be best for us? Are we ignoring the blessings that can come with age? Perhaps our aging is a chance for a more mature appreciation for his gifts and perhaps a slower physical pace that allows us to contemplate all that he does for us.

Even death can be a blessing. It is a release from the pains of this life so that we can be with our God. It also may be a way for God to keep us from sins that would embitter our lives or the lives of others had we lived longer.

Like Hezekiah, we may pray for health and life. God may grant us our request. When he does, we need to use God's answer as an opportunity to appreciate our health as a gift that we do not deserve. Yet, God gives us that gift to use humbly in his service.

## Psalm 88
### Illness as an Opportunity to Draw Closer to God

However, when we are sick our main concern is not serving, but being served. We can see that in several of the prayers about sickness in the Bible. One of them is Psalm 88:

> O LORD God, my savior,
>  I cry out to you during the day and at night.
>    Let my prayer come into your presence.
>      Turn your ear to hear my cries.
> My soul is filled with troubles,
>  and my life comes closer to the grave.

I am numbered with those who go into the pit.

I am like a man without any strength—
    abandoned with the dead,
    like those who have been killed and lie in graves,
    like those whom you no longer remember,
        who are cut off from your power.

You have put me in the bottom of the pit—
    in deep, dark places.

Your rage lies heavily on me.

You make all your waves pound on me.                    *Selah*

You have taken my friends far away from me.

You made me disgusting to them.
    I'm shut in, and I can't get out.
        My eyes grow weak because of my suffering.
            All day long I call out to you, O Lord.
                I stretch out my hands to you ⌊in prayer⌋

Will you perform miracles for those who are dead?

Will the spirits of the dead rise and give thanks to you?    *Selah*

Will anyone tell about your mercy in Sheol
    or about your faithfulness in Abaddon?

Will anyone know about your miracles in that dark place
    or about your righteousness in the place
        where forgotten people live?

I cry out to you for help, O Lord,
    and in the morning my prayer will come into your presence.

Why do you reject my soul, O Lord?

Why do you hide your face from me?
    Ever since I was young, I have been suffering and near death.
    I have endured your terrors, and now I am in despair.
        Your burning anger has swept over me.
        Your terrors have destroyed me.
            They swirl around me all day long like water.

They surround me on all sides.
You have taken my loved ones and friends
far away from me.
Darkness is my only friend!

The writer of this psalm had such a severe illness that he began to think about his death. His illness also became a spiritual struggle. As he felt himself closer to death, concerns about his spiritual well-being and his relationship with God were as important as his physical concerns. He speaks about being as good as dead, coming "closer to the grave," and going "into the pit." (*The pit* is a frequent term in the Old Testament for the place where the dead go.) But notice what he then says:

I am like a man without any strength—
abandoned with the dead,
like those who have been killed and lie in graves,
like those whom *you* no longer remember,
who are cut off from *your* power.

At first, the psalmist appears to be talking about what his extreme illness has done to his relationships with other humans. He is as good as dead and, therefore, abandoned by others and placed in a grave. However, his concern is with his relationship with God. He worries about what death will bring to his spiritual life. Will he be cut off from God? Will he die spiritually as well as physically? What will happen to him eternally when death comes?

That, after all, is the real concern that humans have over death. Will death be the end of everything for us? If it is not, will death bring us something better? Many people, perhaps even most people in Western societies, live as if when this life ends nothing follows. That is why we want all the things we can get in this life.

Polls taken in recent years in the United States show that most people believe God exists. However, behavior of people in our society shows they do not live as if their belief in God means anything practical after death. This life is what counts. We want to feel younger, have more possessions and wealth, and enjoy pleasures of all sorts. Pornography, drugs, moral relativism, and violence pervade our society. One of the reasons for this is the lack of our trust that God can provide for us something other than this life. The most valued ideal for many people in society has become enjoyment of life. That may mean engaging in whatever makes us as individuals happy, feel better, or help us avoid physical, mental, and spiritual pain.

The psalmist was in the midst of that pain. Moreover, he attributed some of that pain to what God had done. He said to God, "Your rage lies heavily on me." He then went on to list the things God had done to bring him pain: God pounded at him with waves of misfortune. God took his friends away and then made him disgusting to them. God shut him in his circumstances with no escape. Later in the psalm he talked about suffering since he was young and always being near death. He complained that God's anger was upon him, and he had been destroyed by terror from God.

The psalmist raised the question of whether God would provide for him after death. Would his sickness lead to death and then nothing? Would he lose the only thing that could possibly endure beyond the grave, his relationship with God?

What we hear in this prayer is a cry for a relationship with God that not only transcends the grave but also addresses the problems of ill health. The two cannot be separated. As we become ill or develop a chronic disease, we cannot separate our present problems from our eternal future.

Is it all right for us to call on God to address our sickness and disease and at the same time express our concern about whether he will provide for us beyond this life? Is the psalmist's prayer a prayer that expresses an unhealthy doubt about God's power? Is it an affront to God and an insult to his divine power? We might read it that way, but I suggest that we would be misreading his prayer.

This prayer is a healthy airing of the psalmist's concerns. As a human he could only imagine what life beyond this world must be like. He could not see it, experience it, or even speak to those who are now enjoying it. His experience could only tell him about this life. If his faith in the promise of God to provide a better life beyond the grave wavered, the healthy thing to do was to raise his concerns and make them part of his prayer. It was better than engaging in behavior that seeks to deny death or numb the pain of life and the effects of ill health. He could have lashed out at his friends. He could have despaired of having any hope and sought to numb his pain with alcohol. Instead, he took his physical, psychological, and spiritual pains to God through his prayer.

Psalm 88 may seem to be a list of doubts and complaints that ends in despair. Instead, it is a healthy spiritual cry for God's help in restoring not only the psalmist's physical health, but also his mental and spiritual health. He openly lays out his concerns. That could only happen as a result of his trust in God.

When we have a chronic disease or even when we are dying, we need to learn to pray as the psalmist did when we are sick. In other words, we need to learn: *Trust in God leads to prayers that are able to bring all of our concerns, pains, frustrations, and worries openly to God.* That is what the writer of Psalm 88 did. We do not know what answer he got to his prayer. But his prayer was preserved for us in the Bible so that we could learn to openly and frankly bring all of our concerns to God, especially when our health fails. The psalmist probably gave us his prayer to show us that true spiritual health trusts God enough to boldly pray about concerns, knowing God will listen. He shows us that God would rather hear our doubts and conflicts than allow our ill health to become a time of losing our spiritual well being.

## Psalm 102
### Illness as an Occasion to Praise God

In Psalm 102 we find another prayer of a person whose health failed. He prayed:

O LORD, hear my prayer,
> and let my cry for help come to you.
>> Do not hide your face from me when I am in trouble.
>> Turn your ear toward me.
>> Answer me quickly when I call.

My days disappear like smoke.
My bones burn like hot coals.
My heart is beaten down and withered like grass
> because I have forgotten about eating.
I am nothing but skin and bones
> because of my loud groans.
I am like a desert owl,
> like an owl living in the ruins.
I lie awake.
I am like a lonely bird on a rooftop.
All day long my enemies insult me.
> Those who ridicule me use my name as a curse.
I eat ashes like bread
> and my tears are mixed with my drink
>> because of your hostility and anger,

because you have picked me up and thrown me away.
My days are like a shadow that is getting longer,
  and I wither away like grass.

But you, O Lord, remain forever.
  You are remembered throughout every generation.
  You will rise and have compassion on Zion,
    because it is time to grant a favor to it.
      Indeed, the appointed time has come.
        Your servants value Zion's stones,
          and they pity its rubble.
The nations will fear the Lord's name.
All the kings of the earth will fear your glory.
When the Lord builds Zion,
  he will appear in his glory.
  He will turn his attention to the prayers
    of those who have been abandoned.
  He will not despise their prayers.
This will be written down for a future generation
  so that a people yet to be created may praise the Lord:
    "The Lord looked down from his holy place high above.
    From heaven he looked at the earth.
      He heard the groans of the prisoners
        and set free those who were condemned to death.
        The Lord's name is announced in Zion
          and his praise in Jerusalem
            when nations and kingdoms gather
              to worship the Lord."

He has weakened my strength along the way.
He has reduced the number ⌊of⌋ my days.
I said, "My God, don't take me now in the middle of my life.
  Your years ⌊continue on⌋ throughout every generation.
  Long ago you laid the foundation of the earth.

Even the heavens are the works of your hands.
They will come to an end, but you will still go on.
They will all wear out like clothing.
You will change them like clothes,
and they will be thrown away.
But you remain the same, and your life
will never end.
The children of your servants will go on living there.
Their descendants will be secure in your presence."

In this prayer the psalmist begins with his call to God. He begs God to listen and to respond quickly. The reason for this urgency is his failing health. He describes his illness as having two effects: it is eating away at his lifetime and his body.

As his ill health continues, his lifetime is being shortened. He speaks of his days disappearing like smoke. It is as if his days vanish into thin air. They are gone and can never be recovered. Later he speaks of his days as being like a shadow that is growing longer. The setting sun at the end of a day causes shadows to become longer and longer. The psalmist's illness has brought him to the twilight of his life. The long shadows tell him that his days are few.

His illness not only eats away his days, but also his body. He is so ill he cannot eat. He has lost so much weight he is skin and bones. Because he cannot eat, he knows his spirit is broken: "my heart is beaten down and withered like grass" (Psalm 102:4a). His illness and broken spirit combine to deprive him of sleep, furthering his illness.

These things in themselves would be enough to make anyone miserable enough to cry out in prayer for deliverance from sickness, but another thing added to the psalmist's misery. His enemies used his sickness as a way to insult him. They used his name as a curse! They gloated over his illness. They must have been saying he deserved his poor health.

Often, when someone suffers a tragedy some people will react by blaming the person suffering. It can even become an excuse for not showing mercy and kindness: "He brought it on himself; he'll have to live with the consequences" can be an excuse to do nothing to help someone who is suffering. When a smoker suffers from lung cancer, emphysema, or stroke, it is easy to blame the victim. We can be less than sympathetic and have an excuse for not being as supportive as we ought to be. Some have used the disease known as AIDS to shun those have contracted it. Since this disease is often transmitted by homosexual behavior, it is easy to bring a moral judgment against AIDS victims, even those who contracted the disease in another way. Some AIDS victims have had to endure not only the shame that many associate with the disease but also unwarranted discrimination in public services and employment.

The psalmist's enemies were using his illness in that way and even going further to find satisfaction for themselves in his illness.

The psalmist's frustration with his illness and the gloating of his enemies led him to his real complaint. He told God, "I eat ashes like bread and my tears are mixed with my drink because of *your* hostility and anger, because *you* have picked me up and thrown me away" (Psalm 102:9-10). His concern over his health was coupled with his concern that God had vented his anger on him and then abandoned him. In his failing health and approaching death he needed to know that although God had allowed him to suffer, God would not be forever hostile toward him.

Then suddenly, the prayer shifts its tone. The psalmist remembers that God is eternal, that God never ceases to be God. Because God is always God, his nature never changes. He is a God of mercy, and the psalmist begins to praise God for his mercy. He remembers that God will have mercy on Zion, that God builds

Zion and is praised in Zion. Of course, the application is not merely to the mountain on which Jerusalem was situated. Zion was the city where God's people worshipped him and prayed to him. By extension, the psalmist pictures God's mercy to all of his people. He proclaims: "He will turn his attention to the prayers of those who have been abandoned" (Psalm 102:17). His prayer then turns into praise for God, who hears the groans of prisoners and rescues people condemned to death. The psalmist may have felt like a prisoner to his disease, but he now could rejoice because he knew that God would not abandon him forever.

Would the psalmist be cured and go on living? His prayer does not tell us. In fact, in the last section of this psalm, he restates that he has been weakened, and his life has been shortened. Yet, in his prayer he found comfort in God who never dies and who will exist even when all of creation ceases to exist. The psalmist may die, but God will continue to be merciful to him and those who come after him. The psalmist ceased to be concerned about whether he would be cured. His prayer led him to the confidence that God was greater than his illness, and that God was greater than anything he could have in this world, even if he lived to be cured. He still prayed that God would not allow him to die in the prime of his life, but he was content to know that God would never cease being merciful.

The prayer we know as Psalm 102 leads us to another lesson about prayers we might pray during sickness or ill health: *Our God is greater than everything in this life. He will outlast our life and our world. During poor or failing health we can praise God because we know he will have compassion on us no matter what the outcome of our disease.*

## Jesus Shows Us How to
## Pray When Our Life Is Ending

Perhaps the ultimate outcome of failing health is death. It is one thing to pray when we are sick, even so sick that we feel as if we are dying. It is another thing to pray when we know that we are dying. What can we pray for then? Of course, we may want to pray for others—our family, our friends—and ask God to watch over them. We may also wish to pray that God would forgive those who mistreated us during our lives. But what are we to pray about for ourselves? Jesus' short prayer on the cross demonstrates how we should pray when dying. Luke tells us, "Jesus cried out in a loud voice, 'Father, into your hands I entrust my spirit.' After he said this, he died" (Luke 23:46).

Jesus had many concerns as he was dying. He was concerned about his mother, and he provided for her (John 19:26). He was concerned about those who persecuted and executed him, and he prayed that they might be forgiven (Luke 23:34). He even had compassion on one of the other men who was crucified with him (Luke 23:43). However, his final thoughts when dying turned to God. He placed himself into his Father's hands. At the point of death we have no one else and nothing else to turn toward. We can only trust in God, or despair of having anything beyond the grave. Jesus shows us that in all of life, and especially in death, our only hope is in God. When health fails for the last time, no amount of medical technology that can prolong our lives is able to match the loving arms of a Father in heaven who is willing to receive us into life with him.

Jesus' prayer has taught other Christians how to pray when their health is failing. We see it again in Scripture when Stephen was dying. Luke tells us, "While council members were executing Stephen, he called out, 'Lord Jesus, welcome my spirit'" (Acts 7:59).

He placed his spirit in the hands of Jesus, who had placed his spirit into the hands of the Father.

But how can we prepare ourselves to face our own death when it comes? We will die but once, so we can't rely on experience. Where will we find the strength to pray like Jesus or Stephen when we are dying? God gives us many chances throughout our lives to practice for the final failure of our health. We can use our times of illness as times of prayer and reflection. We can pray for God to focus our lives on him so that we can be better prepared for the time when we will die.

In addition, we can reflect on the end of life whenever a relative, friend, or acquaintance dies. If that person were a Christian, we can pray that God would help us learn from their example of faith to help guide us when we face death. We can use their funeral as a time to contemplate on the things God's Word says about death and eternal life and pray about them. And we can learn from these experience to place all of life in God's hands so that when death comes we are prepared to pray as Jesus and Stephen did.

When our heath fails for the last time or when we are with someone else who is dying, a short prayer placing our spirits in the hands of Jesus and his Father is enough. The ultimate answer to prayer when health fails is God himself.

The psalms contain many prayers that mention sickness as one of their concerns (for instance, Psalms 38, 39, and 69). I would recommend a study of this topic in the psalms as a way of learning more about praying during illness. Reading through the psalms with this topic in mind will lead you to understand the many things we can pray about in connection with failing health.

# When Family Provides Support

HAT IS THE most significant relationship of adulthood? Some would argue that it is their relationship with their occupation. Much of our adult existence revolves around our job, and we often relate to other people on the basis of what we do. Yet our occupation does not span our entire adulthood or define all of it. We spend our adolescence and early adulthood in education, preparing for our future career. In our current economy many people change employers, jobs, and even careers several times. Few of us end our careers doing the same job. Some may be farmers, physicians, or attorneys for their entire careers, but careers are not that stable. In April 1993, *The Economist* reported that only twenty-five percent of American workers could expect to stay in their present job twenty years or more. That same month, *Money* magazine reported that average job tenure in corporate America had shrunk to less than seven years. In addition, those who live to retirement age often end their career and live a significant portion of their adult life without an occupation.

Those who have children often feel that the most significant relationship of adulthood is parenthood. Parents' lives seem to revolve around their children, feeding and changing diapers when they are young and guiding them through childhood and adolescence to adulthood. Parenting, if done conscientiously, takes time, effort, and dedication. It often brings us friends who have children the same age as our own as we participate in school, civic, or church activities for the benefit of our children. Yet, children grow up and become adults. We may remain their parents, but we are no longer parenting them. Parenthood, though an important part of many adult lives, is not the defining relationship of adulthood.

However, there is one set of relationships that is significant for the vast majority of adults: family relationships. Moreover, the relationship that has been the center of family life throughout human history is marriage. Even those who never get married are affected by it. Most likely their parents were married. If their parents were not married, the lack of that relationship can have profound affects on their childhood, as the current concern over single parent families demonstrates. Therefore, we should also seek to learn what the Bible tells us in its prayers concerning family and especially marriage.

While some live their entire lives without marrying, the overwhelming majority of adults spend their lives as spouses. For those who never marry, the fact that they remain single shapes their lives in many subtle and not-so-subtle ways. Many feel a loss at not having children. This feeling has led some single women to contract with fertility clinics to be artificially inseminated in order to have a child. Increasingly single men and women are filing lawsuits to force adoption agencies to allow them to adopt children, a privilege formerly given almost exclusively to married couples.

Moreover, those who are divorced or widowed are effected by their former marriages in many ways, social, economic and psychological. I have heard several radio news interviews with experts on divorce. In almost every interview these experts point out that divorced women are more likely to live in poverty than married women and that divorced men and women live fewer years on average than their married counterparts.

The marriage relationship is the most sought after voluntary relationship of adulthood. The need for companionship is present for most adults. The Bible depicts God seeing this need in Adam. When God created Adam, he recognized that "'It is not good for the man to be alone'" (Genesis 2:18). This universal need among humans is recognized in our laws and sanctioned by government. The bitter resentment and acrimony that accompanies many divorces are often the mirror image of the support and strength that many marriages offer both spouses. The strength of a marriage often has good effects on the rest of a family, especially children. Any teacher will testify that a strong home life that comes from a good and stable marriage has a positive effect on that marriage's children. A strong marriage helps spouses weather the struggles of life, such as death of parents, siblings, or children; loss of a job; illness; or failing health.

The Bible recognizes the benefits of marriage and presents it as the norm for most adults. Both the Old and New Testaments speak of marriage as God's gift for the benefit of humans. With all of this support for marriage and recognition of its benefits, surprisingly few of the prayers of the Bible speak about marriage. In addition, few are about the blessings of marriage and family. We will examine the few that do exist: Hannah's prayers in 1 Samuel 1:10-13 and 2:1-10 (both set in the context of a spouse who was supportive) and Psalms 128 and 133 which speak of that support coming not only from a spouse, but also from other members of a family. As we examine these prayers we will discover another principle about prayer: God is not only the origin of prayer, but he also supports us so that we can pray. In the prayers we look at in this chapter we will see how God uses spouse and family as part of that support.

## Hannah's Experience:
### Spouses Support One Another in Prayer

Hannah's prayers never mention her husband or her family. Yet both husband and marriage form the basis of the two prayers in 1 Samuel. Hannah's first prayer grew out of trouble in her family and the expectations of society. She was one of Elkanah's two wives. Like many women in the ancient Near East, Hannah tried to live up to the common expectations of wives in her day: to produce children for her husband. However, Hannah had no children. Elkanah's other wife, Peninnah, had several children, both sons and daughters. Although Hannah was unable to have children, the Bible offers us evidence that Elkanah was still devoted to her. When Elkanah sacrificed to the Lord at Shiloh, we read that he not only gave portions of the sacrifice to Peninnah and her children, but that he also gave a portion to Hannah. The Bible tells us that he did this even though the Lord had kept her from having children (1 Samuel 1:5). He did not allow his love for her to depend on what she could do, but he loved and supported her even when she could not do what was expected of a "good wife."

We read that Peninnah tormented Hannah over her lack of children when Elkanah took them to worship at the Lord's house. Peninnah might have been telling Hannah that the Lord was withholding his blessing from her (Psalm 127:3-5; see also Genesis 29:31). So the time spent in sacrifice and worship at Shiloh was a time of misery for Hannah. She felt separated from God and perhaps from her husband, even though he supported her. We can almost hear the disappointment and frustration in Elkanah's voice. When Hannah cried and refused to eat, he asked, "'Hannah, why are you crying? Why haven't you eaten? Why are you so downhearted? Don't I mean more to you than ten sons?'" (1 Samuel 1:8). Elkanah supported Hannah, but she was still downhearted. She could not live up to society's expectations for her.

Despite this, Hannah went to God in prayer. She prayed for a son and promised God, "'Lord of Armies, if you will look at my misery, remember me, and give me a boy, then I will give him to you for as long as he lives. A razor will never be used on his head'"(1 Samuel 1:11). Hannah made a vow to the Lord, a type of vow that is explained in Numbers 6. The person who takes this vow is called a Nazirite. Very specific rules apply to such a person. Nazirites were forbidden to drink alcohol or vinegar or eat gapes or anything made from them such as wine or raisins. They also were forbidden to cut their hair. In the Bible we know of only three Nazirites, all of whom were placed under this oath from birth. Two of them, Samuel and Samson, served as judges of Israel. The third, John the Baptizer, is the only Nazirite mentioned in the New Testament (see Luke 1:15).

The Nazirite was especially dedicated to the Lord. Hannah was showing her devotion to the Lord in her prayer by promising she would raise her son to be loyal to him. Hannah's vow is remarkable because she was willing to dedicate to the Lord the son she wanted so dearly. She would only have her son with her for a short period of his life. Keeping her vow meant that at a very young age her son would leave her. Yet, she was willing to return the Lord's gift to him.

However, Hannah wasn't the only one willing to make this sacrifice. Numbers 30:1-14 tells us that husbands had the right to cancel the vows that their wives made to God. Elkanah never canceled his wife's vow. He supported her even though it required him to give up his son. Elkanah, despite his disappointment and frustration with his wife's depression over not bearing children, sympathized with her. He knew her pain and was willing to sacrifice so that she could keep her vow. Hannah prayed with the confidence she had the support of her husband.

When we think of the benefits of marriage, we might consider many of the blessings of love, support, and comfort that spouses can offer each other. However, we seldom consider how marriage can be a blessing in our prayers. People like Hannah who have the support of their spouses can rely on it in prayer. If our spouse supports us, we can pray about our wants and needs with the confidence that our they will be part of God's plan to supply all that we need. A supportive, godly husband or wife provides added strength to a spouse's prayer. The blessings of being married to a partner who not only is loving but also who loves God translates into spiritual support as we bring our requests to God.

However, the story of Hannah's prayers does not end with her request for a son. After God answered her prayer and provided a son, she returned to God's house to dedicate her son. There she prayed again:

"My heart finds joy in the LORD.
My head is lifted to the LORD.
My mouth mocks my enemies.
    I rejoice because you saved me.

There is no one holy like the Lord.
There is no one but you, O Lord.
There is no Rock like our God.

"Do not boast
⌞or⌟ let arrogance come out of your mouth
because the Lord is a God of knowledge,
and he weighs ⌞our⌟ actions.

"The bows of the warriors are broken,
but those who stumble are armed with strength.
Those who were well-fed hire themselves out for a piece of bread,
but those who were hungry hunger no more.
Even the woman who was childless gives birth
to seven children,
but the mother of many children grieves all alone.

"The Lord kills, and he gives life.
He makes ⌞people⌟ go down to the grave,
and he raises them up ⌞again⌟.
The Lord causes poverty and grants wealth.
He humbles ⌞people⌟; he also promotes them.
He raises the poor from the dust.
He lifts the needy from the trash heap
in order to make them sit with nobles
and even to make them inherit a glorious throne.

"The pillars of the earth are the Lord's.
He has set the world on them.
He safeguards the steps of his faithful ones,
but wicked people are silenced in darkness
because humans cannot succeed by their own strength.

"Those who oppose the Lord are broken into pieces.
He thunders at them from the heavens.
The Lord judges the ends of the earth.

He gives strength to his King
and lifts the head of his Messiah."

(1 Samuel 2:1-10)

This prayer shows us a Hannah in the opposite frame of mind from her first prayer. She prayed her first prayer while she was depressed. It was a short, one sentence prayer of twenty-six words (in Hebrew). Hannah was so upset and downhearted she could hardly find the words to pray. In contrast, Hannah prayed this second prayer when she was joyful.

Her joy is evident from the beginning. She prays about the happiness the Lord has given her and acknowledges that he alone could give her such joy: "There is no one holy like the Lord . . . There is no Rock like our God." That is what we would expect from a person of faith, but in the middle of the first part of Hannah's prayer, we find a disturbing thought: "My mouth mocks my enemies." Hannah expresses some contempt for those who made her feel miserable when she was unable to bear children. (That could have included Peninnah but may also have included others in society who looked down on her when she was childless.) Is she taking the vindication God gave her and turning it into selfish joy and delight? Or, is this attitude something that is proper? The answer to these questions comes in her next thought: "'I rejoice because you saved me'" (1 Samuel 2:1). Hannah's mocking is connected with God's actions.

The prayer goes on to explain why she mocked others. She reminds everyone who speaks arrogantly that the Lord is in charge of all things. The middle of her prayer speaks of the power of God to change the fortunes of humans. He is in control of human strength, life and death, honor and shame. God can transform human situations so that those who are lowly or needy become honored. He can also make those who are powerful weak. He can even give childless women, children and turn the joy of a mother to grief because of her children. Hannah is mocking the arrogance of those who place their trust in human abilities and worldly power and status. That is what Peninnah did. She used her blessing in this world as if they were her own instead of God's. Hannah acknowledged that her son was God's and was willing to dedicate him to God.

Her enemies arrogantly thought that humans controlled their fate. They took advantage of their blessings from God to bring misery on Hannah rather than giving thanks to God and offering comfort and support to her. However, Hannah knew that "humans cannot succeed by their own strength." She mocked those who thought that they could use their strength without God's blessing and in ways he never intended. Her mocking was a reflection of God's attitude toward such arrogance.

The arrogance that Hannah felt bearing down on her when she could not have children was not merely the torture of having to endure the taunts of Peninnah. Peninnah was merely reinforcing what her society already was communicating: that women who could not have children were less than adequate as wives. In our day society has different values about marriage and family. Some of them are in keeping with God's will, but others are not.

For instance, some parents feel inadequate if they cannot provide their children with many luxuries. However, good parenting is more than merely providing the latest toy or game for our children. Supportive spouses who know this do not make each other feel guilty that they cannot give their children things. Good parents give their children the emotional and spiritual gifts that modern western society often overlooks. When spouses support one another, they are led to prayer and find what Hannah found—a God who supports them through their spouses. They find a God who "lifts the needy from the trash heap in order to make them sit with nobles and even to make them inherit a glorious throne" (1 Samuel 2:8).

In examining the circumstances of Hannah's prayer, we have discovered another principle about prayer. In chapter one we discovered that prayer originates with God. Now we learn that *God is not only the origin of prayer, but he also supports us so that we can pray.* That support can come in many ways. In this chapter we see that God supports us through family and especially through spouses. However, this does not mean that those who are not married have less support from God than those who are. Other family members can offer the support we need. Even those Christians who do not have any living family members receive support through their family in Christ, their brothers and sisters in the faith.

Such support is very important, even when we are separated from those who provide it. Though Hannah was not physically separated from her husband Elkanah, she felt isolated from him when she could not bear children. Yet his support helped her pray. Christians who are physically separated from their loved ones often draw on the knowledge that others support them as they pray. Christians have been imprisoned for their faith and have been separated from their loved ones by war or natural disasters. But they still have found strength in knowing that God has others in this world who love them and are concerned for them. We can even find examples of this in the Bible. For instance, when Paul was in prison he wrote to the Philippians:

> I thank my God for all the memories I have of you.
> Every time I pray for all of you, I do it with joy. I can
> do this because of the partnership we've had with you
> in the Good News from the first day ⌊you believed⌋

94

until now. I'm convinced that God, who began this good work in you, will carry it through to completion on the day of Christ Jesus. You have a special place in my heart. So it's right for me to think this way about all of you. All of you are my partners. Together we share God's favor, whether I'm in prison or defending and confirming the truth of the Good News. God is my witness that, with all the compassion of Christ Jesus, I long ⌊to see⌋ every one of you.

(Philippians 1:3-8)

Just as Paul felt the support of his brothers and sisters in Christ as he prayed in prison, we also are supported by God through those whom he has placed around us. Those who have a Christian spouse find that support as part of the special relationship of marriage that God has given to humans.

## *Family Members*
## *Support One Another in Prayer*

When we look at the book of Psalms we find two prayers that tell us about the importance of support from spouse and family. One of these is Psalm 128:

Blessed are all who fear the LORD
and live his way.

You will certainly eat what your own hands have provided.
Blessings to you!
May things go well for you!
Your wife will be like a fruitful vine inside your home.
Your children will be like young olive trees around your table.
This is how the LORD will bless the person who fears him.
May the LORD bless you from Zion
so that you may see Jerusalem prospering

all the days of your life.
May you live to see your children's children.

Let there be peace in Israel!

This psalm is a prayer for blessings for the person who is faithful to God. It wishes blessings of prosperity for everyone who not only believes God's promises, but who also strive to live as God wants. This psalm wishes six blessings for such a person: food provided by labor, a wife who prospers, children who provide blessings, prosperity for Jerusalem, grandchildren, and peace for Israel. Of these six blessings, three come through family: wife, children, and grandchildren. Of those three, wife is listed first. While children and extended family members are important, the value of a good spouse outweighs them all, and the psalmist shows us this by mentioning wife before other family members.

The sequence of blessings in this psalm is not accidental. It is deliberately planned. The psalmist begins by mentioning the blessing of receiving a good reward for labor. This first blessing is one that would enable a person to contribute to a family's well being. By being able to earn enough so that he could feed himself (and perhaps feed others as well), the recipient of this blessing would be a blessing to others. He could have a wife and children. Thus, this first blessing leads to the other blessings.

The next blessing is a spouse—a wife, because the psalm is addressed to a man. The wife is compared to a fruitful vine. The picture of a grapevine filled with grapes was a common one in ancient Israel. Grapes were a major crop. As we do today, ancient Israelites used them as fruit and to produce raisins and wine. As we read this psalm we might immediately think that the comparison of the wife to a fruitful vine speaks of the wife bearing children. While this would be a part of the intended comparison, we shouldn't conclude that it is the sole sense in which the comparison is to be understood. The blessing that a wife brings represents not only children, but also all the other physical and spiritual blessings that a wife can provide for her husband. This is borne out by the other blessings mentioned in this psalm: children and grandchildren are mentioned, but so are prosperity from Jerusalem and peace in Israel. These blessings are primarily spiritual blessings and are part of the blessings wished upon the person addressed in this psalm.

The psalmist's view of a good spouse is not one-dimensional. The husband's contribution is more than support for the family through his labor. The wife's contribution is more than the children she is able to bear. Both contribute to spiritual blessings. The psalmist pictures the wife bearing fruit for the entire household. The blessings that husband and wife give each other include emotional and spiritual blessings for their household. Together they pass those blessings on to their children.

The third blessing, children, follows from the second. The wife not only brings children into the world, but also, with her husband, provides a household where those children can grow, learn, and mature physically, emotionally, intellectually, and spiritually. By picturing the children as young olive trees, the psalmist helps us to anticipate the growth of the children, who are ready to shoot up like young, vigorous olive shoots.

His choice of olive trees is an important one. Olive trees were prized for their fruit which provided an important source of dietary fat for ancient Israelites. Since meat was expensive, not always available, and often reserved for special occasions, olives and olive oil were important foods. Olive oil was an important ingredient in many foods and also served as cooking oil. It allowed average Israelites, who would not otherwise have enough fat in their diet, to remain healthy. The image of children as olive trees pointed toward prosperity and further blessings as the children grew.

Thus, the children are pictured as being blessed by their parents as they grow and as blessings to their parents. Of course, this presupposes a household where the parent's faith in God guides their lives. The psalmist is assuming that the parents provide for their children's religious training. That is why the next blessing he prays for is the Lord's blessing from Zion, the site of the temple. This family provides support for one another because of the faith which mother and father share with their children. It leads them to focus on God, to worship him, and to lift up their prayers to him.

Such faithful people looked for Jerusalem to prosper. Prosperity was not measured with economic factors: profits by Jerusalem's merchants, riches for its residents, a growing economy, and an ever-shrinking lower class. Rather, prosperity for Jerusalem meant that people honored God as they worshipped him in the temple, as sacrifices were brought to him, and prayers were made to him. Throughout the prophecies of the Old Testament and especially in the accounts recorded in the books of Kings and Chronicles, prosperity for Jerusalem was tied to the worship of God. Therefore, the blessing of the family that faithfully worshipped together benefited all of God's people. In turn, a spiritually healthy community was a blessing to that faithful family. Therefore, the psalmist wishes this blessing to last all the days of the life of the person who reads this psalm.

Then the psalmist moves on to another blessing, grandchildren. A third generation who can benefit from the blessings that began with husband and wife is the psalmist's next wish for his readers. Of course, this blessing implies a long life. It also implies that all the blessings of this psalm will endure so the grandparents can rejoice that God gives the same blessings to their grandchildren as he had given to them.

Living long enough to see one's grandchildren may not be perceived as a blessing if those grandchildren are born into a world without hope of prosperity. For the faithful follower of God, living to see one's grandchildren is a blessing if those grandchildren are taught the fear of the Lord that their grandparents have. The implication of this blessing is that the faithful parents had a strong marriage in which the husband and wife supported one another in their life and their faith as they both grew spiritually. Those parents hand their values and faith down to their children who, in turn, hand it on to the grandchildren. The psalmist is not only wishing a blessing of long life for his readers, but he is also wishing them a lifelong blessing. He wishes his readers a strong and enduring marriage characterized by both partners' strong and enduring faith in God.

This leads to the final line of the psalm and its final blessing: "Let there be peace in Israel!" (Psalm 128:6b). Peace among God's people is very important. When God's people are beset with arguments and strife, maintaining one's faith becomes very difficult. It also becomes difficult for families to worship together with God's people if the church has constant bickering and quarrels among its members. Many families have withdrawn from weekly worship services because their congregation had internal clashes. In contrast, the psalmist wishes peace for Israel, God's people (see Galatians 6:16). When such peace exists, all the other blessings of this psalm are enhanced.

However, the Hebrew word *shalom* which is translated *peace* in this verse means more than an absence of hostilities. It also contains the idea of the presence of good and proper relationships among people. That is what the psalmist wants God's people to enjoy. They don't merely cover over their antagonistic feelings, grudges, and prejudices toward one another by making an outward peace that belies inward hostilities; they also live together in true inward peace because they have forgiven one another as God has forgiven them. This type of peace supports Christian families, and those who have such peace support other Christians. Therefore, this psalm begins as a prayer for blessings upon individuals and their families, and ends as a prayer for the entire family of God.

Viewing God's people as a family is an important metaphor used throughout the Bible. It is also an important theme in the last prayer about family life that we will examine, Psalm 133:

> See how good and pleasant it is
> > when brothers and sisters live together in harmony!
> > It is like fine, scented oil on the head,
> > > running down the beard—down Aaron's beard—
> > > running over the collar of his robes.
> > It is like dew on ⌊Mount⌋ Hermon,
> > > dew which comes down on Zion's mountains.
> > > That is where the LORD promised
> > > > the blessing of eternal life.

This psalm speaks of the blessings when family members live together. The Hebrew word translated *brothers and sisters* is the normal word for *brothers*. However, in Hebrew it can mean family members in general and is used of nephews (Genesis 14:14,16), cousins (1 Chronicles 23:22), and other close relatives. It can even refer to women relatives (Deuteronomy 15:12, 2 Chronicles 28:8).

In this psalm it may have an even wider meaning. We might refer to someone who has a close, common bond with us as a brother or sister even though they are not related to us in any way. Similarly, this psalm may be speaking of those who share the common bond of faith in God as brothers and sisters. Paul did the same thing in his letter to his fellow Christians whom he called brothers and sisters.

This psalm may be using the term *brothers and sisters* in the wider sense to denote those who are not siblings. However, we can understand it only if we first understand its implications for actual family members—real brothers and sisters. Then we can begin to understand its extended meaning.

Of course, brothers and sisters don't always live in harmony. Sibling quarrels are a part of this life. There may be conflicts over petty jealousies that parents have to deal with. Or there may be fights over inheritances that can divide brother from brother and sister from sister. However, the psalmist pictures the blessings that come when brothers and sisters are able to live in harmony and put aside their bickering. He compares such harmony with fine, scented oil poured on the head of Aaron, Israel's first chief priest.

The picture of oil poured on a head is not a pleasant one for us, but it was for the Israelites. Olive oil had many uses for the ancient Israelites. It served as food as well as fuel for lamps. Perfumed and scented olive oil was a cosmetic applied to the hair and skin to make them appear healthy and smell pleasant. Often hosts at a party would anoint their guests as a sign of goodwill and favor toward them (see Psalm 23:5). In addition, olive oil was part of special ceremonies to induct people into high offices. In these ceremonies oil was poured on the head of the person inducted into office. This anointing symbolized God's pouring his Holy Spirit out upon the person inducted into office. Thus, we can read about Saul and David being anointed as kings (1 Samuel 10:1, 16:13). In

Leviticus 8:12 we read about Moses anointing Aaron to be chief priest of Israel. It is this anointing to which Psalm 133 refers.

The psalmist uses the picture of anointing in a very interesting way. He begins by saying that the harmony between brothers and sisters is like oil on the head. Perhaps the first thought is that he is referring to the use of oil to beautify and perfume the hair. Then he extends the picture to oil running down on the beard. Perhaps we might now be lead to think of anointing someone for an office. On the other hand, we might still think that this is speaking of perfuming one's head of hair and perhaps also the beard, as at a party. Then he adds that it is running down Aaron's beard and onto his robes. Now we are given the picture of God pouring out his Spirit on Aaron as he becomes high priest.

In his skill as a poet, the psalmist has combined a number of pictures to show us how pleasant harmony among family members is. It reminds us of beauty and sweet perfume. More than that, it reminds us of God's blessing on us when he sends us his Holy Spirit to give us faith and guide us in life. This piling up of pictures powerfully communicates what harmony among family members is. It is something we can appreciate and enjoy as we might enjoy beauty and sweet smells. True family harmony comes from God as he pours out his Holy Spirit on us. It is a gift from God.

Then suddenly, the psalmist switches pictures and speaks of family harmony as dew on Mount Hermon, the highest mountain in the Anti-Lebanon mountain range. It marked the northern limits of Joshua's conquests (Joshua 11:17; 12:1). Because snow covers Mt. Hermon year-round, it serves as a major source of water for the Jordan River. Throughout most of the year the evaporation of water from the snow of its peaks allows dew to form on its slopes. In contrast, the land around Mt. Hermon is arid. In a land where rainfall is critical and water shortages can lead to death of crops, cattle and people, dew is critically important for life. The picture is of an area where life can flourish.

As the psalmist started with one picture of anointing and moved to another, here he also transforms the picture of life-giving dew. It now also falls on the mountains around Zion. They, like Mt. Hermon, enjoy dew. Since Mt. Zion was the location of God's temple, the flourishing life is now transformed from the physical life of plants and animals to spiritual life that only God can give. In fact, the psalmist makes this clear. Zion is where God promised the blessing of eternal life.

We now have a complete picture of the harmony that the psalmist is speaking about. This harmony is shared by those who have eternal life. The family harmony that God wishes all of us to have is not just a pleasant home life, but a harmony that comes from sharing the promise of eternal life with those in our family. The support that husbands and wives can give to one another in Christians homes is founded on the eternal life they share in Christ. The harmony of brothers and sisters who have been taught the promises of God in Jesus and share the faith of their parents is more than the love that non-Christians have for their brothers and sisters. It is a love deepened and enhanced because brothers and sisters share the love of God.

This harmony is then extended to our brothers and sisters in Christ. We can understand better why the Scriptures often speak of Christians in family terms. Because we share one heavenly Father, we can live in peace and harmony with one another. How good and pleasant that is!

We started this chapter with a story about disunity and discord in a family. As we consider the Bible's various prayers about husbands and wives and their families, we can see that God wants us to have unity, harmony, and peace in our families. However, we learn that the only lasting harmony we can have in our families comes from God himself. It begins when a husband and wife share not only their common bond of marriage, but also the bond of unity in Christ Jesus. When spouses support one another in life and in prayer, they pass that support down through their generations so the true peace that only God can establish becomes a part of family life.

# 6

# *When Prayer Becomes Prayer*

 OW SHOULD WE pray? Christians have always sought ways to pray and have wanted to learn how to pray properly. The questions that I have been asked about prayer in my duties as a pastor or when I was a professor at a Christian college usually had to do with the *content* of prayer. I was often asked, "Are certain requests appropriate in prayer?" I have never encountered someone who wanted to ask for something in prayer that they thought was directly against God's will. For instance, I have never been asked whether a request that is clearly against the explicit meaning of the Ten Commandments was appropriate for a prayer. Instead, the request usually questioned whether a certain heartfelt desire was appropriate, or whether it was selfish, and therefore against the spirit of God's law.

These questions about whether we should include certain requests in our prayers are not easily answered. We have already examined biblical prayers in which the requests for punishment of enemies were a central concern. In the last chapter we examined

Hannah's prayer for a child, which certainly was a prayer that included one of her most personal desires. Praying for a heartfelt personal need is not necessarily wrong. Yet, how can we pray for those needs and at the same time not fall into the sin of placing our personal desires above God's will? To answer this question we need to examine some of the Bible's prayers that can serve as models and patterns for our prayers. We will also learn two more important principles about prayer:

1. God's Word, the Scriptures, is the foundation upon which prayers are built.
2. We need to center our prayers on God's promises.

In addition, the Bible's prayers will teach us how to construct our prayers. One question I have never been asked about prayer, but that I suspect lies behind many of the questions I receive, involves the mechanics of prayer. How should I word my prayers? What should I put first? We know to start a prayer with some reference to God and close it with *amen*. However, many Christians feel they do not quite know how to arrange the thoughts and requests they want to include in their prayers. Often, they are reluctant to lead others in prayer. After all, their prayers don't sound like the well-organized prayers that are often prayed during worship services. By examining prayers in the Bible, we can learn about the patterns used in biblical prayers and learn how to compose our own prayers (even as we are praying them).

## Learning From Jesus
## What to Ask for in Our Prayers

Of course, the most familiar prayer intended to serve as a model of Christian prayer is the Lord's Prayer. It is found in two places in the Bible with different forms. In Matthew it is part of the Sermon on the Mount (Matthew 5–7). In Luke we are told that it is Jesus' instruction to his disciples when they asked him to teach them how to pray. The form of the prayer in Matthew is the one prayed by Christians as the Lord's Prayer. Luke's version is slightly differently than Matthew's version. Moreover, the version in Luke omits two of the thoughts found in Matthew's version:

| *Matthew 6:9-13* | *Luke 11:2-4* |
|---|---|
| | Jesus told them, |
| "This is how you should pray: | "When you pray, say this: |
| Our Father in heaven, | Father, |
| let your name be kept holy. | let your name be kept holy. |
| Let your kingdom come. | Let your kingdom come. |
| Let your will be done on earth | |
| as it is done in heaven. | |
| Give us our daily bread today. | Give us our bread day by day. |
| Forgive us as we forgive others. | Forgive us as we forgive |
| | everyone else |
| Don't allow us to be tempted. | Don't allow us to be tempted." |
| Instead, rescue us from | |
| the evil one. | |

## The Opening of the Lord's Prayer: God as Father

Scholars have long recognized that the Lord's Prayer contains seven requests, or petitions. (Luke's version contains only five. We will explore possible reasons for the omission of the third and seventh petitions.) Before giving these petitions, Jesus taught his disciples to address God as *Father*. This was the way Jesus addressed his prayers.[1] Throughout the Sermon on the Mount Jesus referred to God as their Father.[2] While God was occasionally referred to as a father in the Old Testament (Psalm 103:13; Proverbs 3:12), no prayers address him as Father. Jesus is the one who teaches us about our relationship with God as our Father. That relationship brings us to God in prayer, trusting that he loves as a perfect Father who listens to his children's requests and who wants to give them every good thing. In other words, praying to God as our Father focuses us on the first commandment. It reminds us we should have no other gods that we trust (see Exodus 20:3-6).[3] When we pray to God as our Father, we are saying that we trust only him.

The early Christians understood this and prayed to God as their Father. Paul reminded his readers that when they prayed they called on God using the Aramaic word for father, *Abba* (Romans 8:15, Galatians 4:6), just as Jesus did (Mark 14:36). Of course, we have other ways of addressing God in prayer. However, Jesus and Paul both emphasized that when we pray we should understand the close relationship that God has with us. When we receive Christ and all that he has done for us, we become children of God who know his love. This should lead us to pray with the confidence that God wishes to hear our prayers and is always ready to listen to our requests. Moreover, this should make us bold in prayer so that we do not hold back our thoughts and desires from God when we pray. Instead, we can bring all our thoughts and requests to him.

However, Jesus instructs us to pray this prayer together. Individual Christians are not to think of themselves as if they were God's only children and pray "*My* Father." Instead, Christians are to pray together and for the common good. Therefore, Jesus taught his disciples to pray "*Our* Father." While Luke's form of the prayer begins simply "Father," it also assumes Christians are praying for their common good. Luke quotes Jesus as saying, "When you (*plural* in Greek) pray . . ." Moreover, both Matthew and Luke tell us that Jesus taught his disciples to pray "Give *us*," "Forgive *us*," "Don't allow *us*." Calling on God as *our* Father not only reminds us of our relationship to him, but also reminds us of our relationship to each other. If God is our Father, we are brothers and sisters. Jesus instructs us to pray as united family members who have the love of the Father and who love each other.

Moreover, the address to God reminds us that he is our Father *in heaven*. Our relationship with him and, therefore, with our brothers and sisters, is a spiritual one. Jesus is teaching us to pray to our Father in heaven so that we learn that our prayers transcend our earthly limitations. We pray to God in heaven so that the earthly barriers of culture, language, social or economic status, race or age are overcome. Too often we want to identify Christianity with our situation in life. We tend to think of our culture or subculture as somehow embodying Christian characteristics instead of understanding that all human cultures not only contain good but also contain sinful traits and characteristics. In the United States, churches have often been polarized along racial lines. Instead of praying "Our Father," we can at times be praying "My Father (and the Father of those like me)." Yet, Jesus reminds us that he came for people of all races and cultures, of all languages, of all ages, and of all classes. Earthly divisions are not relevant when we pray to our Father in heaven.

## THE ORGANIZATION OF THE SEVEN PETITIONS:
## FOCUSING ON WHAT IS IMPORTANT

When we come to our heavenly Father, what should we ask for? As we turn to the seven petitions of the Lord's Prayer, we find that the first three focus on God's work in our lives. The fourth petition focuses on our physical needs, the only one to speak of any needs for our bodies. The fifth, sixth, and seventh petitions are requests for our spiritual well-being. Jesus is showing us how to construct our prayers so they emphasize our spiritual needs. Because Jesus understood the situation of humans in this world, he knew they tend to be most concerned with their physical needs. He saw this in the many people who followed him looking for cures for their diseases. He felt the pressure to make him their king because he could provide them with unlimited food (John 6:15).

We are no different from the people in Jesus' day. Our primary concerns are most often for the physical things we need. We live in a world where we cannot separate ourselves from our constant physical, from the air we breathe, to the shelter we sleep in, to food we eat, to the clothing we wear, and to the things we possess. Our physical needs overwhelm us to the point that they often crowd out the most important needs in our life, our spiritual needs. That is why in the Sermon on the Mount Jesus followed this prayer with warnings about concentrating on our physical wants and needs. He warns us about the difficulty of being both rich and a Christian (Matthew 6:19-24). He tells us that life is more than our physical needs (Matthew 6:25-34). In addition, he shows us how to construct our prayers so that we do not dwell on our physical needs and neglect our greater spiritual needs. He shows us to begin by asking for things that we know our heavenly Father wants to do for us and to end with requests for spiritual blessings. He does not deny our need for physical blessings, but shows us that they are nothing without the spiritual blessings from heaven.

### THE FIRST PETITION: HONORING GOD'S NAME

What are the things that our heavenly Father wants for us? In the first petition Jesus teaches us to pray, "Let your name be kept holy." At first this may not seem like something our Father wants for us, but for him. However, God's name is holy by its very nature. What is not holy is our use of it. In this petition Jesus is telling us to pray we might be given the strength to keep God's name holy. How can we do that?

The obvious way is to not use God's name in such a way that he is dishonored. We shouldn't speak evil of God or use his name in ways that would bring him a bad reputation. Examples are teaching in God's name anything that is not true, anything that is intended to deceive others, or anything that is used to cover up a lie such as false testimony under an oath sworn in God's name.

However, we are also praying that God would move us to use his name correctly. We are asking that we do not merely avoid using God's name incorrectly, but that we learn to use it correctly (as in praying to him). This is an important point, especially for the Jews who first heard Jesus. You see, by Jesus' time, in order to avoid misusing God's name the Jewish people quit using the name God had used to identify himself in the Old Testament. God's name, *Yahweh*, ceased to be pronounced by Jews. Instead they substituted the Hebrew word for *Lord*. (That is why in many Bible translations *Yahweh* is translated by LORD [in small capital letters] while the Hebrew word for *Lord* is translated Lord [only the first letter capitalized]). The Jewish people thought they could avoid misusing God's name if they did not pronounce it. However, God did not give us his name so we would neglect using it out of fear of misusing it. Instead, he wants us to use his name; to call him God, Father, and Lord, and to teach others to use it correctly.

Speaking God's name is not the only way we can use or misuse his name. The way we live is also included in this petition. We are praying God would teach us to live holy lives so that when others see us they praise the God whom we believe in and serve (Matthew 5:16). When we Christians do not live holy lives, but do things that even non-Christians know are wrong, we can bring ridicule to God and shame on him and his name.

In the first petition we ask God to keep his name holy in our lives as well as in our speech. In other words, Jesus teaches us to pray that God would give us the strength to keep the second commandment and honor his name (see Exodus 20:7).

## THE SECOND PETITION: GOD'S KINGDOM AMONG US

The second petition is a request for God's kingdom to come. In many places the Bible speaks about this coming of Jesus as king to usher in God's eternal kingdom. Peter urged his readers to look forward to that coming of God's kingdom (2 Peter 3:10-13). Jesus is telling us to pray for that kingdom to come so that it remains our constant hope.

However, God's kingdom also comes in another way. Both John the Baptizer and Jesus told the people of their day that the kingdom of God was near (Matthew 3:2; 4:17). Later, Jesus told the Pharisees that the kingdom of God was among them (Luke 17:21). Paul told the Colossians that they had been brought into God's kingdom (Colossians 1:13). God's kingdom will come in glory at the end of time, but it also comes to us today in the Good News about Jesus. In this prayer we pray that God's kingdom continues to come to us and others through God's Word. We are asking that God would make us able to hear his promises and believe so that we can be members of his kingdom now.

Therefore, this second petition is a prayer that God would help us keep the third commandment (Exodus 20:8-11). While that commandment speaks mainly about honoring the Sabbath as a day without work, the Sabbath was never understood as only a day for rest. It was always seen as a day to hear God's word and be strengthened in faith through that word of God. Jesus endorsed that view of the commandment by preaching in synagogues on the Sabbath (e.g., Luke 4:31).

Jesus did things on the Sabbath that could have been considered work. He cured diseases and approved of other things his disciples did on the Sabbath, such as harvesting wheat for a meal (Matthew 12:1-8). Some thought that Jesus and his disciples were breaking the Sabbath. However, Jesus never spoke against worship on the Sabbath, and he frequently used the Sabbath to bring the good news of God's kingdom to others. He kept the true spirit of the Third Commandment.

Of course, Jesus does not tell us to pray, "Let your kingdom come on the Sabbath." He teaches us to pray for God's kingdom to come without any limitation to a particular day. In this prayer he tells us to ask our heavenly Father to send his kingdom constantly. Whenever the promises of God's word are read, heard, or used, this prayer is being answered.

### THE THIRD PETITION: A SUMMARY OF THE PRAYER THUS FAR

The third petition asks that God's will would be done. It acknowledges that God's will is done in heaven. We request God's will be done on earth in the same way it is done in heaven. But how is God's will done? An easy and quick answer might be God's will is done whenever people live according to his law. Of course, God wants people to live holy lives. However, if we view this request as a prayer that God rigidly enforce his law, quickly punishing anyone who breaks it, we would be misunderstanding what this petition is asking. God does not desire for people to be forced to live according his law. He wants them to live according to his law because they want to live that way. God wants us to do his will out of love for him as our heavenly Father (the introduction). He wants us to live lives that bring honor to his holy name (the first petition) as grateful members of his kingdom (the second petition). Therefore, in the third petition when we ask that God's will be done, we are summarizing our prayer to this point. (Perhaps this is why Luke's version does not contain the third petition. Jesus omitted it when he privately taught his disciples how to pray. Since the third petition summarizes the first two petitions, it can be omitted without changing the meaning or focus of the prayer.)

However, we also acknowledge some important truths as we summarize the first part of our prayer. First, we acknowledge that God's name is holy in heaven. That is, those who have gone to heaven before us now live holy lives that honor God's name. As we acknowledge this truth, we look forward to the time when we will join them and be freed from our failures to bring honor to God's holy name.

Second, we acknowledge that God rules in heaven and that we are looking forward to living in his glorious kingdom with him as our king. That is, we are longing for the best of all governments: when God rules over us and when we can see the full glory of our king. Because of our human failings, we have never lived under a government that is perfect and enjoys the support of all its citizens.

However, in this petition we acknowledge that a perfect government does exist and that we are eager to become its citizen. God has made us members of his kingdom already in this life when he gave us faith in our Savior. We pray in the third petition of the Lord's prayer that we are longing to live under the full power and glory of that kingdom as those Christians who are now in heaven.

Therefore, as we close the third petition, we have prayed that God would enable us to keep the first part of his law—that we love him with all our heart (Matthew 22:37). In the Ten Commandments, the first three tell us what God expects of those who love him.

## The Fourth Petition:
## All That We Need to Live in This World

The fourth petition of the Lord's Prayer requests daily bread. Here in one sentence Jesus teaches us to ask for everything we need in life: food, clothing, shelter, possessions, family, friends, health, peace, and any other good thing that is a part of this life. Jesus summarizes all our earthly needs and puts them in the only petition to ask for the non-spiritual concerns of life. While Jesus minimizes the needs that we often feel most, he does not overlook them when he teaches us to pray. On the contrary, as a human being he was acutely aware of our physical, psychological, and social needs. He knew hunger (Matthew 4:2) and thirst (John 19:28). He had family and friends whom he loved (John 19:25-27; 11:3). So he teaches us to pray for these things.

However, he includes those needs in only one petition of the Lord's Prayer. Since we feel the need for these things in this life so acutely, we often make these our major concerns and allow them to crowd our spiritual needs out of our thinking. Jesus provides a balance by minimizing our prayers about our daily bread.

Yet, when Jesus tells us to pray for these things, he reminds us that our heavenly Father does provide all the needs of life. As we pray for these things, we are praying God would make us aware that he does provide us everything we need every day. If we know God provides them for us, we will not have to break any of the last seven of the Ten Commandments. Those commandments are concerned with our relationships with other people. They command respect for those in authority (Exodus 20:12), for the human life (Exodus 20:13), for marriage (Exodus 20:14), for property (Exodus 20:15), and for others' reputations (Exodus 20:16). They also forbid sinful desires as well as sinful acts (Exodus 20:17). When we realize that God gives us all that we need for our body and life, we do not have any need to break these commandments. In the fourth petition, we pray that God would make us thankful for the daily bread that he gives to all people. He even gives it to those people who do not have faith and do not pray for daily bread (Matthew 5:45).

### The Fifth Petition: Acknowledging Our Failures

By the time we come to the fifth petition of the Lord's Prayer, we have already prayed for all our needs according to the Ten Commandments. What is the next thing to pray about? As we pray and ask God to help us to keep his commands, we realize we have not kept them. Every day we stray from his commands. Not everything we do honors his name. We overlook the many ways in which God gives us our daily bread, and we forget to give thanks for it. Therefore, we need to beg our Father for his forgiveness for our failures. That is exactly what Jesus tells us to do in the fifth petition.

As we pray the Lord's Prayer and meditate on its meaning, we are moved to realize we can receive all these things only if our relationship with our heavenly Father, daily broken by our sin, is daily re-established. In the fifth petition we ask God to re-establish it. In pleading with him to forgive us we acknowledge we cannot restore that relationship. We must rely on him to keep his promise to forgive us. Jesus tells us to pray for forgiveness so that we never fall into despair and think that God will not forgive us. He teaches us that we can believe God's promise and rely on him to love his children so much that he is always ready to forgive them.

Moreover, Jesus reminds us that sin not only breaks our relationship with God, it also breaks relationships we have with others. Those who sin against us are in need of forgiveness, and Jesus teaches us to forgive others as our Father forgives us. He already taught his disciples that those who show mercy in forgiving others are blessed, because they will be shown mercy (Matthew 5:7). Jesus tells us that in our prayer we should promise God to restore the broken relationship we have with others because of their sins against us. He urges us to take the first step in healing wounded relationships in the same way our Father heals our wounded relationship with him.

### THE SIXTH PETITION: POWER TO OVERCOME SIN

In the sixth petition, our Lord teaches us to pray that we would not be tempted, so that we can avoid sinning. After recognizing our sins, we pray that God would keep out of our lives any temptation that would lead us to sin. However, we are not merely asking God to keep us out of situations where we might feel the urge to sin. We are asking him to strengthen us so that we can resist temptation.

## The Seventh Petition:

## A Summary of the Fifth and Sixth Petitions

Finally, in the seventh petition, Jesus teaches us to pray that God would keep the Evil One, Satan, from gaining control over us through our weakness, through desires for things in the world, or through any other of the tools he uses to draw people away from God. Although the Lord's Prayer is traditionally prayed, "Deliver us from *evil*," the Greek text of Matthew says, "Rescue us from *the Evil One*," using a term for the devil elsewhere in Matthew (5:31; 13:19, 38). Jesus is teaching us to pray that God would always keep us out of the power of the devil and his temptations. Satan is treated here as the ruler of this world who wants to bring all kinds of evil into our lives. Therefore, Jesus wants us to pray that God would guard us from all kinds of evil, especially sin, by keeping us safe from the crafty enemy of our souls.

This last petition of the Lord's Prayer is a summary of the fifth and sixth petitions. In those petitions, we pray for forgiveness, promise to forgive others, and pray that we are not tempted to sins. In other words, we are praying God would keep us from all evils that could plunge us back into spiritual death. We pray for forgiveness so that we don't fall into despair that God has abandoned us because of our failures. We promise to forgive others so that we do not deny them the forgiveness that God has given us and turn them away from Christ. Finally we pray that God would not allow anyone or anything to tempt us. These evils can destroy our souls, and the devil is always trying to use them to separate us from our heavenly Father. Therefore, Jesus adds a summary petition to remind us exactly how seriously they can damage us. Now we can understand why this petition is missing from Luke's version of the Lord's Prayer. Just as Jesus omitted the third petition without changing the thrust or meaning of the prayer, so he omitted the seventh petition without altering its meaning.

Now that we have examined the Lord's Prayer, we can appreciate it as a well structured and deeply meaningful prayer. Jesus teaches us to pray for the important things in our life by structuring the first part of the prayer (introduction through the fourth petition) on the Ten Commandments. He shows us how to pray for the spiritual power we need so that we can live according to God's will. Then in the second part of this prayer (the fifth, sixth, and seventh petitions), he teaches us to pray about our failures and our weaknesses. We ask that we will overcome the evil powers of this world that want to prevent us from using the spiritual power that God freely gives his children.

## Learning from Jesus to Pray Our Own Prayers

The masterful construction of the Lord's Prayer is part of its power that has moved Christians throughout the centuries to adopt it as a prayer for use in public worship and private devotions. However, Jesus did not teach his disciples this prayer only for repeating word-for-word. He did not want us only to pray the Lord's Prayer, but also to learn from it so that we can grow in composing our own prayers.

Can we learn to construct our prayers in the same way? I believe we can. In fact, for hundreds of years the Christian church has used a similar construction in its prayers. In many churches a prayer known as a *collect* (pronounced *có-lect*) is said each Sunday before the reading of the Scriptures. These prayers are designed to focus the worshippers who are gathered together (Latin *collectus*, "gathered") on the theme of the Scripture readings for that day.

Most collects follow a simple, but powerful, pattern:

1. The invocation (an address to God)
2. A description of God or of one of his acts that reflects the content of the prayer
3. The petition (a request)
4. The benefit hoped for as a result of the granting of the request
5. A closing, often mentioning the Trinity (Father, Son, and Holy Spirit)[4]

As we look at prayers in the Bible, we can find that many of them contain the first three elements of the collect. The Lord's Prayer follows that pattern: Invocation ("Our Father"), Description ("who is in heaven"), and the seven petitions. In addition, although Jesus did not include a closing for the prayer, the Lord's Prayer is often said with a closing ("for thine is the kingdom, and the power and the glory forever and ever").[5] Jesus not only taught his disciples a prayer, he gave them a pattern to follow when praying. The church has used that pattern throughout its history. It is an easy pattern to use. This way we can focus our thoughts on our prayer and not be distracted by things around us. If we learn to pray in this way, we can grow in constructing even our most impromptu prayers so that they focus our thoughts clearly and effectively on our concerns, needs, and desires.

For instance, if we wanted to pray for children to be brought to faith in the Savior, we could compose a prayer using the collect pattern or the pattern we find in the Lord's Prayer. Our prayer might be:

Lord Jesus (*introduction*), you taught your disciples not to prevent little children from coming to you, but to bring them to your loving arms (*description*). We ask that you would call all children to faith (*petition*) so that they would know the joys of your love (*benefit*). This we ask in your name. Amen (*closing*)

When we use this type of organization for our prayers we find four benefits. First, it focuses the thoughts of our prayer by helping us to organize our prayer from beginning to end. Second, it focuses us so that we do not stray from the things we feel a need to pray about, and our prayers don't end up as a disconnected list of wishes and wants. Third, it helps us to meditate on the Scriptures as we pray. When we include a description of God or something he has done, we draw on what we know about him from the Bible. Our prayer becomes a means of thinking about and applying what we have read in the Scriptures. Finally, following this or another pattern in prayer helps us make our prayer true prayers. That is, our prayers become spiritual exercises that draw us closer to God and his word. That is what Jesus was teaching his disciples. When we learn to pray as Jesus taught his followers, we stop going to God with a disjointed, rambling list of self-centered needs and requests, and prayer becomes prayer.

## Learning to Pray from Other Prayers in the Bible

However, the Lord's Prayer is not the only prayer in the Bible that serves as an example for us to imitate. Once we have learned the lessons that Jesus teaches us in the Lord's Prayer, we can search the Scriptures to find other examples to guide us as our prayer life grows and matures.

## Ezra Reminds Us to Remember God's Promises When We Pray

In the book of Ezra we find a short prayer that the people prayed when the temple's foundation was laid:

> As they praised and gave thanks to the LORD, they sang antiphonally: "He is good; his mercy toward Israel endures forever."
>
> (Ezra 3:11a)

This short prayer of praise to God contains two descriptions of God. It tells us that he is good and reminds us that God never does anything that is not good. Then it draws a conclusion about God—that his mercy endures forever. This prayer not only brought glory to God but also encouraged the people. As they praised God for his mercy, they encouraged one another to rely on his mercy and to not lose heart when hardship or sorrow entered their life. This prayer, of course, was not new. It was sung earlier in history. It was part of the prayers when David brought the ark to Jerusalem (1 Chronicles 16:34, 41). It was sung again when Solomon dedicated the first temple in Jerusalem (2 Chronicles 7:3, 6). Through Jeremiah the Lord promised that it would be sung again in Jerusalem (Jeremiah 33:11). It also is the basis of Psalms 106, 107, 118, and 136.

This short prayer is an excellent example of a powerful prayer that has inspired God's people to pray and meditate. In Psalms 106 and 136 it serves as a framework for reviewing God's mercy throughout the Israelites' history. From its example, we learn that a short, well-crafted prayer can be as powerful as a long one. Our prayers are heard not because of the number of words we speak or because of lofty phrases that touch the hearts of those who pray with us, but because of the content. This prayer points to a central truth about God: that he has promised to be merciful without limit. That alone makes it powerful.

When we pray, we need to learn to center our prayers on God's promises. That is what can make our prayers powerful in their effect on us and on others. We may not always choose eloquent words or be able to express all the thoughts of learned theologians. Nevertheless, our prayers can be moving and meaningful if they simply center on God's promises. That is what this one short biblical prayer did.

### AGUR TEACHES US TO EXAMINE OUR LIVES BEFORE WE PRAY

Another short prayer that can teach us how to pray is Proverbs 30:7-9:

> I've asked you for two things.
> Don't keep them from me before I die:
> Keep vanity and lies far away from me.
> Don't give me either poverty or riches.
> Feed me ⌊only⌋ the food I need,
> or I may feel satisfied and deny you
> and say, 'Who is the LORD?'
> or I may become poor and steal
> and give the name of my God a bad reputation.

This prayer by Agur is remarkable in that it closely mirrors some of the thoughts in the Lord's Prayer, especially the fourth and sixth petitions. Agur's two requests of God are personal in nature. The first, like the sixth petition of the Lord's Prayer, is a prayer that he would not be tempted. However, this request is more specific than the sixth petition. It requests that God would not allow him to be tempted to speak lies or other words intended to deceive people.

Agur's second request is that God would not allow him to become too poor or too rich. Agur explains why he makes this petition. If he becomes too rich and can count on always having an abundance of food (and possessions), he might be tempted to forget God. He might think that he can get along without his Creator. If he becomes too poor, he might be tempted to steal to provide for his needs. This would reflect badly on God's name, since Agur claims to be a follower of God. Therefore, Agur's second petition is not only a request that God would give him his daily bread (the fourth petition of the Lord's Prayer), it is also a request that God would not allow circumstances to tempt him to sin and deny God (the sixth petition) or bring shame on God's name (the first petition).

Why did Agur pray for these two things? The answer to that question is in his explanation of his second request. Agur understood himself well. He knew he was prone to certain types of sin. While we are all sinful, not all temptations to sin are equally powerful temptations for each person. One person may be more likely to commit one type of sin, whereas the temptation for another type of sin is more appealing to a different person. Agur understood his temptation to misuse wealth. He prayed that God would help him with that temptation.

Agur's prayer teaches us that we need to examine our lives before we pray. What are our needs? They may be different from the needs others feel. What are our strengths and weaknesses? They may not be the same strengths and weaknesses others have. When we pray together with others we may want to pray for a general deliverance from temptation. When we pray by ourselves, we should pray especially for those things that apply to ourselves.

However, to pray such prayers, we need to learn about ourselves. We need to examine our lives and learn what spiritual challenges we face and need help in overcoming. Agur did that and could pray about his needs. We cannot pray as he did unless we take the time to know ourselves and the spiritual struggles that we face every day. This is a difficult spiritual exercise because we often deny our faults and failures. We deny them so well that we overlook them ourselves. However, prayer becomes true prayer—spiritual exercise that draws us to God—when we have first examined ourselves in the light of God's word as Agur did. Then we pray with trust in God's promises in the Scriptures as Ezra did.

### Jesus Applied the Insights from Ezra and Agur in His Prayers

As we gain insights into ways of enhancing our prayers, we then need to apply those insights as we pray. It is not enough to learn some theoretical knowledge about prayer; we must also put that knowledge to work, otherwise it will be lost. Most of us know this from personal experience. In high school or college we study many subjects that enable us not only to train for a career, but also to become a well-rounded person. However, in many cases we have forgotten much of the details of what we learned in subject areas we don't use often. Unless our career is in the area of life sciences, we probably have forgotten most of the details of our high school biology class. We may remember dissecting that frog and have a general acquaintance with the basic concepts of biology. However, most of us could not remember the chemical process by which DNA controls the development of an organism, the number of human chromosomes, or many other detailed topics we covered in biology class.

In the same way, if we are to retain the lessons we learn from the Bible's prayers, we need to use them. One prayer of Jesus clearly shows that he applied the lessons that can be drawn from Ezra's and Agur's prayers. It is the prayer of Jesus on the night before he was crucified (John 17:1-26). As Jesus opens his prayer, he speaks about his Father and himself. This part of his prayer shows that Jesus understood himself and what he had done in this world:

> "Father, the time is here. Give your Son glory so that your Son can give you glory. After all, you've given him authority over all humanity so that he can give eternal life to all those you gave to him. This is eternal life: to know you, the only true God, and Jesus Christ, whom you sent. On earth I have given you glory by finishing the work you gave me to do. Now, Father, give me glory in your presence with the glory I had with you before the world existed."
>
> (John 17:1b-6)

Jesus' prayer goes on to make requests for others, but its foundation is this first section. It shows that Jesus clearly knew his needs and the things that he needed to do. He brought them to the Father in prayer. His prayer teaches us to do the same.

In this chapter, we have learned many things about prayer. As we examined the Lord's Prayer, we saw that it is a model prayer that teaches us how to pray. We also looked at other prayers that can serve as examples. As we examined these prayers, we have discovered two important truths. First, we learned that *God's Word, the Scriptures, is the foundation upon which prayers are built.* In the Scriptures, we learn about our relationship to God. When we examine ourselves against its teachings, we can learn the personal spiritual challenges that we face so we can pray to God about the things we really need. Second, we learned that *we need to center our prayers on God's promises.* No matter how much self-examination we do, only God's promises can give us the assurance that we are his beloved children and move us to pray. When we apply these lessons about prayer, our prayers become real prayers.

Any number of prayers in the Bible can serve as guides for our prayers. Besides the prayers examined in this chapter, you may want to look at a variety of psalms from this perspective. I would suggest Psalms 18, 25, 26, 42, 61, 72, 119 (the longest prayer in the Bible), and 141.

# 7

# *When God Receives Praise*

*HILDREN REQUIRE MUCH* attention and have an endless supply of requests. They rely on parents, grandparents, teachers, and others to supply them with the physical, emotional, spiritual support, and guidance they need to grow into mature adults. If parents do their job correctly, their children learn to be thankful for the things others do for them. When they are young, we have to train children to say "Thank you" to someone who has given them something or done them a favor. As they grow older, they learn to realize they should be thankful and learn how to express that thanks without having to be reminded. Expressing our thanks is something expected of those who understand the favors others have done for them.

Although we teach our children to give thanks to others, we do not often teach them another equally important practice: praising others. Even as adults, we find it is difficult to praise a person who has done something well. Praising them makes us feel a little uncomfortable. We are much more likely to praise them to others, though the persons who are being praised often do not hear it. Therefore, children seldom praise their parents for what they have done in providing a home and an education for them. This is unfortunate, since giving well-deserved praise is an important way of showing how deeply grateful we are to the dedication and excellence they brought to their responsibilities or obligations.

Unfortunately, this reluctance to praise can lead to a deficit in our prayers. We may praise God less in our prayers than we ought. Like children who know to thank their parents, but are reluctant to praise them, we can become people who thank God for what he does, but fall short of praising him. Thanks and praise go together. However, praise goes beyond gratitude for what God has done to recognition of the unsurpassed excellence of everything God does. It not only shows our gratitude, but it also shows our appreciation for God's nature and his works.

Prayers of praise in the Bible fall into two broad types. One is praise for God that urges others to praise him also. The other type is praise that glorifies God's attributes or actions. Many prayers contain both of these types. As we examine both types of praise we will learn two important lessons:

1. We can and should praise God for the many things that he is and does. However, the greatest motivation for our praise for God comes from his love and compassion for us in his Son.
2. Since our entire relationship with God is founded upon Christ, our praises always build upon his work for us.

# Psalm 150
## Calling on Everyone to Praise God in Every Way

The last psalm, Psalm 150, contains mainly the first type of praise.

Hallelujah!

Praise God in his holy place.
Praise him in his mighty heavens.
Praise him for his mighty acts.
Praise him for his immense greatness.
Praise him with sounds from horns.
Praise him with harps and lyres.
Praise him with tambourines and dancing.
Praise him with stringed instruments and flutes.
Praise him with loud cymbals.
Praise him with crashing cymbals.

Let everything that breathes praise the Lord!

Hallelujah!

The word *Hallelujah* is a combination of two Hebrew words: *Hallelu* (praise) and *Yah* (the shortened form of God's name, Yahweh). This psalm, like Psalms 111, 112, 113, 135, 146, 147, 148 and 149, begins by calling on God's people to praise him. However, this is not the ordinary way for calling on someone to praise God. The word *hallelujah* occurs only in the book of Psalms. This way of calling on people to praise God is reserved for worship. It specifically speaks to God's people gathered to worship him. Therefore, it calls for praise for God from those who understand his mercy and goodness toward them.

Except for the beginning and ending hallelujahs, Psalm 150 consists of ten sentences calling on people to praise God. The first one calls on people in his holy place to praise him. That is, it calls on the people assembled in the temple to sing his praises in worship. The second one calls on everyone in heaven to praise him. Thus, all of God's people, not only those we see around us, but all those who have gone before us, are urged to praise him.

Sentences three and four are the only two in this psalm that give a reason for praising God, and they do that in the most general terms. We are urged to praise him for who he is and for what he has done. This prayer does not elaborate on what God has done, nor does it dwell on any particular attribute of God for which we are to praise him. It leaves those things to the worshippers to contemplate. They may think of things he has done for them as a group. Or they may contemplate the many different things he has done for them as individuals. They may praise him for all of his wonderful attributes, his power, knowledge, wisdom, glory, and so on, or for particular attributes they appreciate at the moment of praise.

The next six lines urge us to praise God in a particular way: with music. Among the musical instruments mentioned are horns, harps, lyres (stringed instruments similar to harps), tambourines, flutes, and cymbals, along with various stringed instruments as well as dance. This psalm reminds us that prayers can be sung as well as spoken. Hymns often serve the function of prayers sung by groups of worshippers.

From ancient times God's people have used music as an important part of their worship of God. Christians have always employed music in their worship, composing hymns in each generation, and handing the best of them down to the generations that followed. Part of that musical tradition has been praying to God in song, often accompanied by instruments. This ancient prayer of praise reminds us that some of our most important prayers make use of a marvelous gift that God has given to humans: music. It reminds us that we use not only our minds and our folded hands[1] to praise God in our prayers, but that we also use our entire bodies, including our vocal cords. Musicians who lead the sung prayers may use their arms and hands, legs and feet, lips, mouth, and breath in praise to God (see the last line of the psalm). Those who sing may use their bodies as they stand or kneel. During prayer we can and should use our body to praise God, and we should use the great gift of music as part of our praises.

During my times of prayer I have often found that singing a hymn to God is a powerful way to praise him, even when I am alone. This psalm urges us to make use of the gift of music as part of our regular practice of prayer.

However, music in worship and prayer is not an end in itself. While music has the power to beautify our prayers and deeply touch our souls, it is no substitute for the content of our prayer. That is why the psalmist urges God's people to praise him for his works and his greatness before he encourages them to praise him with music. Music for its own sake is not praise for God. Music with a message about our God and all he has done for us is.

## Psalm 148
### Calling on All Creation to Praise God

Praising God with music is only part of the message of the Bible's prayers of praise. Psalm 148 gives us another view of praise for God.

Hallelujah!

Praise the LORD from the heavens.
Praise him in the heights above.

Praise him, all his angels.
Praise him, his entire heavenly army.
Praise him, sun and moon.
Praise him, all shining stars.
Praise him, you highest heaven
  and the water above the sky.
Let them praise the name of the LORD
  because they were created by his command.
He set them in their places forever and ever.
He made it a law that no one can break.

Praise the LORD from the earth.
Praise him, large sea creatures and all the ocean depths,
  lightning and hail,
  snow and fog,
  strong winds that obey his commands,
  mountains and all hills,
  fruit trees and all cedar trees,
  wild animals and all domestic animals,
  crawling animals and birds,
  kings of the earth and all its people,
  officials and all judges on the earth,
  young men and women,
  old and young together.
Let them praise the name of the LORD
  because his name is high above all others.
    His glory is above heaven and earth.
He has given his people a strong leader,
  someone praiseworthy for his faithful ones,
    for the people of Israel, the people who are close to
him.

Hallelujah!

Like Psalm 150, the praise for God in Psalm 148 consists mostly of calls for others to praise God. It has two parts. The first part calls on everything in the heavens to praise God. Not only are God's heavenly creatures, the angels, called on to give God praise, but also heavenly bodies and even the clouds in the sky are encouraged to praise God. That may seem a little strange to us. We can identify with choirs of angels praising God in heaven, but how do the sun, moon, and stars praise God? Yet, the concept of God receiving praise from his creation is not isolated to this psalm. Psalm 19:1-4 tells us:

> The heavens declare the glory of God,
> and the sky displays what his hands have made.
> One day tells a story to the next.
> One night shares knowledge with the next
> without talking,
> without words,
> without their voices being heard.
> ⌊Yet,⌋ their sound has gone out into the entire world,
> their message to the ends of the earth.

God's creation tells of his glory and praises him without having to say a word. When we contemplate the starry skies at night and when we marvel at the wonders of the universe that God created, we cannot help thinking of his glory. Silently the clouds roll overhead, and the stars, sun and moon pass by. Yet, their testimony to God, who placed them in the heavens and controls their movements, is as loud as any praise God receives. In fact, that is why Psalm 148 calls on us to praise God: He created the heavens and he controls everything that happens in them.

The psalm moves on to call on the earth to praise God. The ocean and its creatures, the weather and its powerful storms, the mountains, plants, and animals are all told to praise God. This part of God's creation also testifies to his power and glory. All of these things should remind us of God's glory. The weather, which we can (sometimes) predict but cannot control, reminds us of God's might with every powerful storm. The wonderful, yet delicate, balance of animal and plant life, that we can so easily destroy through environmental mismanagement, reminds us of God's wisdom in ordering our world better than we can. He deserves our praise, and observation of his world should tell us that.

But the psalm does not stop with the other creatures around us. It calls on us to praise God. It calls on important people (kings, officials, judges) as well as all others to praise God. Moreover, it tells us to praise God two reasons. One is his glory to which heaven and earth testify every day, as the psalm has already reminded us.

The other reason is that God has given his people a powerful leader and defender. The word translated *strong leader* in the above psalm is the Hebrew word for *horn*. It is often used to signify power in the Scriptures. Many animals, such as sheep, goat, cattle, and deer use their horns as part of their power to defend themselves and their young. The psalm uses the horn as a figure of speech to symbolize the strength God gives to his people. In Psalm 132:7 the horn is used as a symbol of a leader to come from King David's family. Here it is used to speak of a powerful leader for God's people.

The Gospel of Mark recognizes the strong leader spoken of in Psalm 148 as Jesus. Mark tells us that when Jesus rode into Jerusalem on the first Palm Sunday, the people shouted, "Hosanna in the highest heaven" (Mark 11:10). The Greek phrase for "in the highest heaven" matches the ancient Greek translation of the Old Testament in only one place, Psalm 148:1. Christians recognize that the strong leader God gives his people is Jesus, the horn from

David's family. Therefore Psalm 148 calls on the people of God, God's true Israel (Galatians 6:16), those who are close to him by faith, to praise him because of the work of the promised Savior.

This final emphasis in Psalm 148 leads us to an important principle about prayers of praise: *We can and should praise God for the many things that he is and does. However, the greatest motivation for our praise for God comes from his love and compassion for us in his Son.*

## Psalm 111, Revelation, and Daniel: Praising God for Who He Is and What He Does

Praise for God's love and compassion shown in his saving work for us is found in a number of psalms. One example is Psalm 111:

Hallelujah!

I will give thanks to the LORD with all my heart
    in the company of decent people and in the congregation.
The LORD's deeds are spectacular.
    They should be studied by all who enjoy them.
His work is glorious and majestic.
His righteousness continues forever.
He has made his miracles unforgettable.
    The LORD is merciful and compassionate.
He provides food for those who fear him.
He always remembers his promise.
He has revealed the power of his works to his people
    by giving them the lands of other nations as an inheritance.
His works are done with truth and justice.
    All his guiding principles are trustworthy.
        They last forever and ever.
        They are carried out with truth and decency.

He has sent salvation to his people.
He has ordered that his promise should continue forever.
　His name is holy and terrifying.
The fear of the LORD is the beginning of wisdom.
Good sense is shown by everyone
　　who follows God's guiding principles.
His praise continues forever.

Unlike the first two prayers of praise we have considered, this psalm does not consist mainly of calling on others to praise God. Instead, it consists of praise that glorifies God and his attributes. It starts with a brief thanks to God and continues with praise for the many things God does and is. It praises God for his great and wondrous works, including the miracles he has done. It praises him for providing for the daily needs of his people, especially their food. It praises him for his truth and justice, especially for the principles that he gave to his people to guide them. All of these are important reasons for praising God and should be part of our praise to God.

However, we should notice woven throughout the praises in this psalm are praises for his love, mercy, and compassion in saving us. Verse four describes God as merciful and compassionate. Verse nine reminds us that he sends salvation to his people. And twice, in verses five and nine, this psalm reminds us that God keeps his promises, the foremost of which was his promise to send the Savior into the world. Like Psalm 148, this psalm centers its praise on God's compassion for his people.

When we turn to the pages of the New Testament, we find the praise for God's mercy in Jesus is seen even more clearly in the praises in Revelation. In the fifth chapter where Jesus is introduced as the Lamb, we read a prayer of praise offered by God's people in heaven:

"You deserve to take the scroll and open the seals on it,
  because you were slaughtered.
You bought people with your blood to be God's own.
  They are from every tribe, language, people, and nation.
You made them a kingdom and priests for our God.
  They will rule as kings on the earth."

(Revelation 5:9-10)

This praise centers squarely on Jesus' sacrifice on the cross. He is praised because he died. The praise then builds because of the consequences of Jesus' death on the cross. His blood bought people from all over the world to be God's own. This praise gives Jesus all the credit for bringing people to God. We cannot claim to have contributed anything to our status before God because Christ did all the work. Nor can we praise ourselves for the status we have in God's sight as members of his kingdom and as priests who serve him (see Exodus 19:6; 1 Peter 2:9). Jesus made us these by his sacrifice. Even the final sentence, "They will rule as kings," is really praise for Jesus because it is his work that makes us royalty.

This praise is followed by two more prayers. These also direct us to Jesus' death on the cross as the major reason for our praise for God:

"The lamb who was slain deserves to receive
  power, wealth, wisdom, strength, honor, glory, and praise."

(Revelation 5:12)

"To the one who sits on the throne and to the lamb
  be praise, honor, glory, and power forever and ever."

(Revelation 5:13)

The last of these prayers is especially important. This is praise for Jesus because he was the Lamb who was offered as a sacrifice for the whole world. But this is also praise for God the Father, the one on the throne. He also is praised for the death of Jesus. He was willing to give up his Son to a horrible death so we could have life. Both the Father and the Son share the praise for the compassion and mercy they showed us at the cross on Calvary.

How different these prayers of praise are from those we are often tempted to pray. We often praise God for the good things he does for us in this life. When something happens in our life that we consider good (restoring of health, a new job or promotion, the birth of a child, the marriage of a son or daughter), we might find an occasion to praise God. These are proper things to praise God for. However, they pale in comparison to the death of Christ for us. If our praise to God is *only* for things in this life, it is not much in the way of praise. After all Paul reminds us, "If Christ is our hope in this life only, we deserve more pity than any other people" (1 Corinthians 15:19). However, if our praise is coupled with our praise to God for saving us from sin and death, if our praises for things in this life presuppose and build upon praise for Christ's sacrifice on the cross, then we have learned how to pray true biblical praises.

The praises in Revelation build on the cross of Christ. In chapter 15, we find another prayer of praise. It is the praise of all who win the victory over evil:

"The things you do are spectacular and amazing,
   Lord God Almighty.
The way you do them is fair and true, King of the Nations.
   Lord, who won't fear and praise your name?
      You are the only holy one,
         and all the nations will come to worship you.
            because they know about your fair judgments."

(Revelation 15:3-4)

The Greek word translated *judgments* is not primarily speaking of judgment against sin and sinners, a judgment of condemnation. Instead, it is a reference to God's judgment of acquittal of sinners for Jesus' sake. It is speaking about God's judgment that sets aside our well-deserved punishment because Jesus has suffered our punishment for us on the cross. His judgment and the work of his Son are the spectacular and amazing things to which this prayer refers. His decision to give us life through Christ is what is praised as fair and true. And that is why people fear him and come to worship him.

Thus, while this prayer of praise does not specifically mention the work of Christ, it is built upon it. Our praises should be built on that same foundation. Sometimes they will explicitly mention the work of Christ to free us from sin. Other times they may presuppose it as their foundation. This is a lesson about prayer we should always remember: *Since our entire relationship with God is founded upon Christ, our praises always build upon his work for us.*

In this light we can understand the prayers of praise of the Bible. One example is the prayer of Daniel when God gave him the ability to tell King Nebuchadnezzar what the king had dreamt and what it meant. Nebuchadnezzar had threatened Daniel with execution if he could not tell him. When Daniel was shown the dream and its interpretation, the first thing he did was to praise God. He could have chosen to go to the king and tell him the dream and then, after the danger had passed, praised God. Instead, Daniel praised God first. His faith in God, who through the coming Savior would make him part of the eternal kingdom of God (Daniel 2:44-45), caused him to praise God before doing anything else. That prayer, Daniel 2:20-23, praises God for his wisdom and power:

"Praise God's name from everlasting to everlasting
  because he is wise and powerful.
He changes times and periods of history.
He removes kings and establishes them.
He gives wisdom to those who are wise
  and knowledge to those who have insight.
He reveals deeply hidden things.
He knows what is in the dark,
  and light lives with him.
God of my ancestors, I thank and praise you.
  You gave me wisdom and power.
  You told me the answer to our question.
  You told us what the king wants to know."

God gave Daniel wisdom so he could tell the king what he wanted to know. Daniel's wisdom, however, was greater than knowing how to interpret a dream. It was a Christ-centered wisdom that led him to praise God.

## The Song of the Three: How God's People Learned to Praise Him

The examples of biblical prayers we have seen in this chapter have taught us how to praise God in our prayers. That lesson was learned also by the people of long ago. As I close this chapter I would like to offer you another ancient prayer composed by God's people. This prayer is found in the ancient Greek version of Daniel. Although it is not part of the original Hebrew and Aramaic, it is nevertheless a wonderful prayer of praise to God. In Greek it comes immediately after the three young men, Shadrach, Meshach, and Abednego (also known by their Hebrew names, Hananiah, Azariah, and Mishael) were thrown into the blazing furnace for refusing King Nebuchadnezzar's order to worship an idol (see

Daniel 3). The ancient writer imagined these young men praising God in the midst of the fire with this prayer, called the Song of the Three, as God's angel protected them from the flames. This prayer draws on many of the praises to God found in the Old Testament. It shows us that from ancient times God's people learned to pray by reading and studying the prayers in the Bible:[2]

You are praised, Lord God of our ancestors,
and you are worthy of praise and supreme honor forever.

Moreover, your glorious and holy name is praised
and it is worthy of supreme praise and supreme honor
throughout every age.

You are praised in the temple where your holy glory is,
and you are to be supremely praised with songs and
supremely glorified forever.
You are praised as you look into the depths of the earth
as you sit on the angels,[3]
and you are worthy of praise and to be glorified forever.
You are praised as you are on the throne of your kingdom,
and you are to be praised with songs and supreme honor
forever.
You are praised in the sky,
and you are to be praised with songs and glorified forever.

All things that the Lord has done, praise the Lord.
Sing his praise and give him supreme honor forever.
Heavens, praise the Lord.
Sing his praise and give him supreme honor forever.
All angels of the Lord, praise the Lord.
Sing his praise and give him supreme honor forever.
Water above the heavens, praise the Lord.
Sing his praise and give him supreme honor forever.

All powers of the Lord, praise the Lord.

Sing his praise and give him supreme honor forever.

Sun and moon, praise the Lord.

Sing his praise and give him supreme honor forever.

Stars in heaven, praise the Lord.

Sing his praise and give him supreme honor forever.

Thunderstorms and dew, praise the Lord.

Sing his praise and give him supreme honor forever.

All winds, praise the Lord.

Sing his praise and give him supreme honor forever.

Fire and heat, praise the Lord.

Sing his praise and give him supreme honor forever.

Winter's cold and summer's heat, praise the Lord.

Sing his praise and give him supreme honor forever.

Frost and cold weather, praise the Lord.

Sing his praise and give him supreme honor forever.

Dew and snow, praise the Lord.

Sing his praise and give him supreme honor forever.

Nights and days, praise the Lord.

Sing his praise and give him supreme honor forever.

Light and darkness, praise the Lord.

Sing his praise and give him supreme honor forever.

Ice crystals and falling snow, praise the Lord.

Sing his praise and give him supreme honor forever.

Flashes of lightning and clouds, praise the Lord.

Sing his praise and give him supreme honor forever.

Earth, praise the Lord.

Sing his praise and give him supreme honor forever.

Mountains and hills, praise the Lord.

Sing his praise and give him supreme honor forever.

Everything that grows in the ground, praise the Lord.

Sing his praise and give him supreme honor forever.

Seas and rivers, praise the Lord.
Sing his praise and give him supreme honor forever.
Springs, praise the Lord.
Sing his praise and give him supreme honor forever.

Whales and everything that swims in water, praise the Lord.
Sing his praise and give him supreme honor forever.
Every bird in the air, praise the Lord.
Sing his praise and give him supreme honor forever.
All wild animals and cattle, praise the Lord.
Sing his praise and give him supreme honor forever.

All people, praise the Lord.
Sing his praise and give him supreme honor forever.
Israel, praise the Lord.
Sing his praise and give him supreme honor forever.
Priests, praise the Lord.
Sing his praise and give him supreme honor forever.
Servants of the Lord, praise the Lord.
Sing his praise and give him supreme honor forever.
Spirits and souls of those who have his approval, praise the Lord.
Sing his praise and give him supreme honor forever.
Holy people and those who are sincerely humble,
    praise the Lord.
Sing his praise and give him supreme honor forever.

Hananiah, Azariah and Mishael, praise the Lord.
Sing his praise and give him supreme honor forever
    because he has rescued us from hell.
    He has saved us from the power of death
    He has released us from the blazing flames and
        freed us from the fire.

Give thanks to the Lord because he is good,
    because his mercy endures forever.

Everyone who worships the God of Gods, sing his praise
   and thank him
   because his mercy endures forever and ever.

For over two thousand years God's people have learned to offer him prayers of praise by reading the Bible and adapting its praises. We can grow in this aspect of our prayer life by doing the same.

The book of psalms contains many prayers of praise. I would recommend that for additional study you begin with the last group of psalms, those that begin and end with *Hallelujah*. Of those, Psalms 146, 147, and 149 have not been treated in this chapter.

## *8*

# *Making Prayer Part of Your Life*

N THE PREVIOUS seven chapters we have looked at the Bible's prayers for desperate times and times of prosperity, times of trial and temptation, and times of joy. What we have not done is look at what the Bible says about prayer. Instead, we have looked at actual prayers and learned from them important lessons to guide us as we pray. In this last chapter I want to offer some suggestions for further Bible study on the topic of prayer. These suggestions can help you grow in your understanding of prayer and in your actual practice of prayer.

A number of approaches to studying prayer in the Bible can be fruitful. The use of a concordance[1] will help. Look up words such as *pray, prayer, thank, thanksgiving, song, hymn,* and *praise.* However, finding these words will not necessarily make for a good study of prayer in the Bible. In the New Testament alone, these words occur in over 150 verses. You will have to sharpen and narrow your study to progress in learning what the Bible says about prayer. After you find the words, you may want to study them in groups:

1. Study those passages that instruct us how to pray, when to pray, what to pray for, etc. For instance, Jesus teaches about prayer in Matthew 5:44 and 6:5-18. Paul tells his readers to pray in Ephesians 6:18-20 and Colossians 4:2-4. Passages such as these tell us much about what to pray for and how to pray.

2. Study passages that tell us about people in the Bible praying. Many of these do not include the prayers themselves, but they tell us when and why God's people in the past prayed. From their examples, we can learn much about prayer. Look for when, how, and why people prayed. If you include study of words such as *thank* and *praise* you can learn about special types of prayer while studying these passages. In addition, a few passages serve as negative examples, showing us how not to pray (Mark 12:40).

3. Study passages that describe prayers offered by God's people. Paul often describes his prayers (e.g., Romans 1:9; Ephesians 1:16-23; Philippians 1:3-11). Others also describe their prayers or the prayers of others. These descriptions are valuable in helping us understand not only what Christians in the past have prayed about, but also why they prayed. We can receive insight into their motivations to pray and their reflections about the prayers they pray.

4. Continue to study prayers in the Bible. This is perhaps the most difficult way to study prayer in the Bible, but I

also believe that it is the most rewarding. By studying the actual prayers of the Bible, we are forced to ask questions such as: Why was this prayer prayed? When was it prayed? How do the prayer's various parts work together to bring the concerns of the person praying before God? Are several concerns or topics evident in this prayer, and how do they relate to one another?

These questions are often automatically answered for us in the first three ways to study prayer in the Bible that I have listed. Only by studying the prayers in the Bible are we forced to wrestle with the setting, occasion, and content of the prayer. When studying many of the psalms, we can only guess at the setting or occasion of the prayer from studying its contents. In other cases the setting and occasion are given, but studying the prayer itself will give us a better appreciation for them. In addition, only by studying actual prayers in the Bible can we discover various ways of composing and structuring our prayers.

As you study prayers, keep in mind some of the most important lessons we have learned. Prayer from beginning to end is dependent on God and his promises. As Christians we acknowledge that we can only understand the promises of God by knowing Jesus Christ and what he has done for us in his life, death, and resurrection.

Finally, practice constructing prayers from the examples in the Bible. Use the concepts, words, phrases, and even sentences of biblical prayers and incorporate them in your prayers. Learn about the occasions that prompted others to pray, and pray in similar circumstances in your life. Moreover, learn to use all of your Bible study to guide you in prayer. We can use everything we learn in the Bible, even when we are not specifically studying about prayer, to guide us to offer richer, more effective prayers. As you do these things God will guide you by his Word so that you will be able to make prayer an essential and regular part of your life.

This approach to a growing prayer life has enriched my life. It has opened up all of the Scriptures as a resource for my prayers. I can include a wide variety of the thoughts, words, and phrases provided by God himself in the Bible. Moreover, it enables me to avoid becoming bored and tired of my own prayers. Instead I can constantly incorporate the new insights God provides as I read the Scriptures and meditate on their potential to teach me how to pray. This is especially important for me, because as a pastor I am often called upon to pray with others and to lead them in prayer. However, you do not need to be a pastor to apply this book's lessons to your life. All you need is a Bible and a desire to learn the lessons it teaches us in the prayers recorded in its pages.

# Notes

## Chapter 2
### When Evil Is Winning

1. Among them are Psalms 3, 4, 5, 7, 11, 12, 14, 17, 30, 31, 35, 43, 54, 55, 56, 58, 59, 62, 64, 69, 70, 71, 73, 74, 86, 94, 109, 129, and 140.

## Chapter 6
### When Prayer Becomes Prayer

1. See Matthew 11:25-26; 26:39 (or its parallels in Mark 14:36 and Luke 22:42), 26:42; Luke 10:21; 23:34, 46; John 11:41; 12:27-28; 17:1-25.

2. See Matthew 5:16, 45, 48; 6:1, 4, 6, 8, 14, 15, 18, 26, 32; 7:11, 21.

3. The Ten Commandments are numbered in two different ways. (The Bible never numbers the commandments.) The numbering I use counts three commandments in Exodus 20:1-7 (or its repetition in Deuteronomy 5:6-15) and seven commandments in Exodus 20:8-17 (or its repetition in Deuteronomy 5:16-21, counting verse 17 as two commands against sinful desires). The alternate numbering counts four commandments in Exodus 20:1-7, counting verses 3 and 4 as separate commands, and six commandments in Exodus 20:8-17.

4. Not all collects contain all five of these features.

5. Although the closing of the Lord's Prayer is included in the familiar King James Version of the Bible (first published in 1611), it is not present in the oldest Greek manuscripts of Matthew and is not present in any manuscript of Luke. Among the manuscripts of Matthew that do include it, its wording varies considerably. The words themselves do not come from Jesus, but they are based on a biblical prayerthe oldest Greek manuscripts of Matthew and is not present in any manuscript of Luke. Among the manuscriptded in an attempt to make the prayer come to a less abrupt ending when used in worship.

## Chapter 7
### When God Receives Praise

1. While the most common custom in the modern western world is to fold hands while praying, the ancient practice was to lift up arms and hands during praying. (For example, see Psalm 28:2 or Psalm 63:4.)

2. The following text is my translation of Septuagint Daniel 3:52-90.

3. Or "cherubim."

## Chapter 8
### Making Prayer Part of Your Life

1. A concordance is an alphabetical list of words that occur in the Bible. Under each word are listed occurrences of the word by book, chapter, and verse. Often a short context line includes a portion of the verse in which the word occurs to help you see how it is used. Some Bibles include short concordances in the back. Longer, complete Bible concordances are available in bookstores and libraries.

# Index of Scripture Citations

# *About the Author*

NDREW STEINMANN is an active Christian who shares his faith with others through his teaching, preaching, and writing.

An adjunct professor at Ashland University, Dr. Steinmann's areas of interest and research include textual criticism of the Old Testament, apocalyptic literature, and the formation of the Old Testament canon. For four years he dedicated himself to a new, contemporary English translation of the Bible, *God's Word*.

Currently, Dr. Steinmann lives in Cleveland, Ohio, with his wife and two children. He serves as the staff pastor at Lutheran Home, a nursing home in Westlake.